ROCKHURST COLLEGE LIBRARY

0 0006 0095449 9

D1029246

Financial Ratios and
Investment Results

Financial Ratios and Investment Results

And the Principle of Strategy Before Selection in Portfolio Management

Donald M. Peterson

Lexington Books
D.C. Heath and Company
Lexington, Massachusetts
Toronto   London

Quotations from SECURITY ANALYSIS: PRINCIPLES AND
TECHNIQUES by Graham, Dodd, and Cottle, copyright 1962,
McGRAW-HILL BOOK COMPANY, are used with permission of
McGraw-Hill Book Company.

Library of Congress Cataloging in Publication Data

Peterson, Donald M
    Financial ratios and investment results.

    Bibliography: p.
    1. Investments. 2. Speculation. 3. Risk. I. Title.
HG4521.P43   332.6   74-16634
ISBN 0-669-96586-3

Copyright © 1974 by D.C. Heath and Company

All rights reserved. No part of this publication may be reproduced or trans-
mitted in any form or by any means, electronic or mechanical, including
photocopy, recording, or any information storage or retrieval system, without permission in writing from the publisher.

Published simultaneously in Canada.

Printed in the United States of America.

International Standard Book Number: 0-669-96586-3

Library of Congress Catalog Card Number: 74-16634

HG
4521
P43

16.00

February 1975

Baker + Taylor

87104

To my wife, Shirley;
to my daughters, Katie and Sarah;

and to the many people
who like to throw darts
at the *Wall Street Journal*

Contents

List of Figures

List of Figures

List of Tables

Preface

It is sometimes said that theory enables one to cope with reality. This study, however, is concerned with how well reality conforms to theory. Perhaps the tone of this study was best described by Raymond Saulnier, Columbia University, who remarked: "Nothing like a few facts to fit the theory."

This study considers the empirical evidence linking some commonly used financial measures with risk-adjusted returns from common stocks. It looks at the price-earnings ratio, growth in earnings per share, dividend yield, growth in dividends per share, payout ratio, total invested capital, rate of return and the debt to capital ratio. Indeed, it is these measures which are often used by security analysts as well as by academics in evaluating the worth of a firm.

But the critical element here is to look at risk-adjusted returns; and it is only recently with the advent of "portfolio theory" and the capital asset pricing model that we now have some idea of how to measure risk-adjusted returns. This one concept makes this study possible; without it, meaningful conclusions would be impossible. Accordingly, we must now recognize that portfolio selection is a two-parameter problem encompassing both risk and return rather than just return as often thought.

Thus the task before us is to use the theory developed in normative decision-making—that is, how to construct an efficient portfolio, to examine the relation between certain commonly used financial measures and risk-adjusted returns from common stocks. Is there, in fact, useful information in financial ratios? Or should one accept the conclusions of the random-walk hypothesis that financial ratios by themselves are void of predictive value?

The answers to these questions are complex but necessary. If security analysis is to continue as a useful profession, some effort must be made to refute the notion that "throwing darts" is a valid selection procedure. And it is the contention of this study that one of these efforts is to rethink the use of financial ratios in evaluating securities.

Acknowledgments

I wish to express my sincere appreciation to Edward R. Lehman, C. Canby Balderston, and Reynolds M. Sachs—all of the American University, Washington, D.C.—for their assistance and counsel in this study.

Second, I am grateful to Richard Foss, Perry Sporn, and Charles Robbins, all vice-presidents of Marine Midland Banks, Inc., New York City, and to Robert Irwin, president of Niagara Share Corporation, Buffalo, New York, for their interest and ideas as this study progressed. Not to be forgotten in this respect are the many security analysts at Marine Midland Banks and elsewhere who provided practical knowledge in the art and science of equity valuation.

Third, for assistance in computer technology and in financial theory, I am most indebted to Robert A. Levy, president of Computer Directions Advisors, Silver Spring, Maryland.

And finally, I am indeed grateful to the developers of Beta theory, including William Baumol, Michael Jensen, Harry Markowitz, William Sharpe, Jack Treynor, and others who contributed to the measurement technique which made this study possible.

Financial Ratios and Investment Results

1 Introduction

Hypothesis

The hypothesis of this study is that certain commonly used financial measures or ratios generally known to the financial community have no inherent value in determining risk-adjusted returns from common stocks. This hypothesis, if true, suggests that stock prices are determined only by future events, thereby supporting both the broad form of the random-walk hypothesis and its related efficiency of the marketplace.[1]

The Problem

Two schools of thought have emerged in recent years concerning common stock valuation. At one extreme are proponents of the broad form of the random-walk hypothesis who argue that historic data have no relevance in predicting stock prices. Their rationale is that only future events are relevant to future prices and that all past information has been fully discounted in the current price of the stock. At the other extreme are financial analysts who rely entirely on historical data and financial measures in appraising the value of a particular common stock. They argue that the existence of principles, or rules of thumb, in investment analysis leads to investment performance superior to that of a random selection. In between these two approaches is the majority of analysts who rely on financial measures and historical data to obtain an overall impression of the worth of a company and then use other subjective valuation techniques, including intuition, in deciding whether or not to recommend the sale or purchase of its common stock.

The dilemma one encounters then is which approach should be followed in attaining superior investment performance. Should the analyst spend his time interpreting financial measures calculated from historical data and try to develop meaningful "rules of thumb," or should he accept the implications of the random-walk hypothesis, ignore historical data, and look only to the future? Or are both approaches necessary? While it is tempting to compromise the dilemma by accepting both approaches, it is also useful to point out that evidence to date (as presented later) has not supported the superiority of such a compromise.

1

There are essentially two ways of testing the superiority of one approach over the other. First, one can examine the investment performance of security analysts who rely entirely on publicly available financial measures for their investment decisions. Their performance can then be compared with that of security analysts who spend their time predicting events and on estimating the impact of these events on future prices. Unfortunately, analyzing the performance of these two groups of security analysts is not possible because very few analysts practice one approach to the exclusion of the other.

Second, one can examine the historical relation between changes in common stock prices and various financial measures commonly used by security analysts. If no relation exists, then either isolated financial measures are not useful by themselves in predicting changes in common stock prices, as hypothesized in this study, or the wrong financial measures were used in the test. This study relies on an empirical examination of the relation between financial measures and returns, but as data on security analysts' performance and their decision processes become available, the first approach may gain more acceptance.[2]

In either case, an assumption made by investors who rely on the services of professional investment advisors is that these professionals are skilled forecasters. Evidence to date, however, suggests that this assumption is not necessarily valid. For example, the performance of mutual funds has not been superior to that of the market averages;[3] the recommendations of brokerage firms appear to be no more reliable than that of random selections;[4] the narrow form of the random-walk theory and tests of filter rules, with some exceptions,[5] tend to discredit the technician;[6] and, the naive estimates of growth rates, perhaps the main determinant of stock price returns, turn out in some cases to be more accurate than those of financial analysts.[7] While this evidence in no way suggests that superior analysis by some individuals does not result in superior performance, it does question whether or not investment advisors and portfolio managers as a group of professionals have properly serviced their clients. And in a broader context, it questions whether or not security analysis, as it is currently practiced, is properly structured and formulated.

But much progress has been made in the academic community regarding the nature of security prices and its effect on security analysis. This progress is most evident by the fact that the random-walk hypothesis has at least been identified and classified. First, there is the *weak* form, which merely states that the current price of a stock fully reflects all information found in its historical price movements. According to this weak form, analyzing past prices—as practiced by technicians—is not a profitable approach to security selection. Second, there is the *broad* or *semistrong* form, the concern of this study, which suggests that all public information is reflected in the current price of the stock. As such, analyzing this public knowledge, including annual reports, dividend increases, historic earnings and so forth, will not result in superior investment performance. And, third, there is the *strong* form of the random-walk hypothesis, which suggests that not even those with full-time professional analytical staffs, for example, mutual fund managers, are capable of attaining superior investment results.

In summary, then, this study provides additional insight into the nature of the random-walk hypothesis and its implications for security analysis and portfolio management. This insight is in the form of empirical evidence which describes the relation between selected financial ratios or measures and risk-adjusted returns from common stocks. Its end purpose is to help portfolio managers and security analysts appraise the risks and rewards of investments in common stocks and to guide them in allocating their time and efforts toward achieving superior results.

Other Related and Supporting Issues

The Dual Nature of Risk and Return

First, while there have been many studies on the relation between financial measures and returns from common stocks, very few of these studies consider the dual nature of risk and return. Risk must also be considered because the investor's objectives are to maximize returns at minimum risk rather than to maximize returns only. If measures of both risk and return are considered, the results of prior studies may be seriously misleading. For example, while prior studies may show that stocks having a low price-earnings ratio generally give higher returns, one must also consider that these higher returns are associated with higher, perhaps excessive, risks. Similarly, while studies may show that stocks of companies having a relatively low payout ratio generally experience superior price appreciation, one also must consider that an investment in these stocks may generate higher risk.

In this regard, recent advances in risk measurement suggest that returns of a well-diversified portfolio, for example, one having perhaps fifteen or more securities with low co-variances, are primarily a function of "market" or "non-diversifiable" risk as measured by the Beta statistic, the least-squares slope of the line regressing portfolio returns against market returns. In contrast, the standard error of estimate is a measure of "unique" or "diversifiable" risk. In the remaining chapters, the Beta statistic and the standard error of estimate are given for each of the financial ratios subjected to empirical study. In addition, various composite, one-parameter measures are shown as indicators of risk-adjusted performance, that is, including both risk and return.

But while the Beta statistic as a measure of market risk and the standard error of estimate as an indicator of unique risk have certain limitations (see Chapter 2), the real problem in measuring performance is finding a more suitable statistic. The Bank Administration Institute, for example, recommends the use of the mean absolute deviation of returns as a proxy for risk.[8] Other possibilities include the standard deviation, semivariance, quartile ranges, and other statistical measures of stock price variability. Variability of earnings could also be considered as a measure of risk under the assumption that this variability is ultimately reflected in the fluctuations of the price of the stock.

Fact versus Fiction in Security Analysis

A second supporting problem is that textbooks on security analysis are replete with statements and propositions without evidence. Walter Muhlbach has stated the problem as follows:

Until we clean out the sixty years' accumulation of misconceptions and useless formulae in our stable of analytic tools we shall be continually hampered in the performance of our analytical responsibility. This is our goal.[9]

It is against this lack of empiricism and "useless formulae in our stable of analytic tools" found in textbooks used by students that this study should be beneficial. It is no longer sufficient to state, for example, that low P/E stocks offer defensive characteristics unless evidence is presented to support this contention.

Design of an Information System for Security Analysts

A third supporting problem is that the information-gathering system of a security analyst or portfolio manager should be designed depending on the validity of the random-walk hypothesis. Consider the following three possible situations.

First, if the broad form of the random-walk is correct in that all historic, publicly available information is irrelevant to future prices, then investment analysts should design a system which will maximize the quantity and quality of "private" information available to them. This private information could be in the form of company visits, informal discussions with top management, or contacts with other financial advisors who have access to private information. While these sources of private information are certainly sought after, it is questionable whether or not certain types of information can properly and legally be used without discrimination against the non-institutional investor. If it is shown that only future events determine future prices, and if the policy of the SEC is to forbid analysts from seeking and using private information, then the role of the analyst is indeed limited.

Second, if past events, both qualitative and quantitative, are relevant to future stock prices, then the role of the analyst is to identify these events and to weigh them accordingly. His role then becomes meaningful as an "interpreter" of these events.

And, third, if financial measures or ratios calculated from historic financial data are closely related to stock price behavior, then the analyst's role becomes one of emphasizing the quantitative aspects of investment analysis. In this case, quantitative methods, computer screens, and/or man-machine interactive systems could dominate the investment decision. And if lags do exist in the processing of new information, then capital markets are not efficient since the prices of stocks do not respond immediately to all available public information.

Each of these three situations requires different weights on historic versus future information as well as on qualitative versus quantitative methods. As one searches for evidence refuting or confirming the broad form of the random-walk theory, one can systematize his information-gathering techniques and rethink the weights placed on each factor.

Generating an "Efficient Portfolio"

A fourth supporting problem is that the relation between selected financial ratios and returns from common stocks is important in providing inputs to the "efficient" diversification of stocks in a portfolio.[a] While traditional portfolio management depends upon risk minimization via industry diversification, portfolio theory emphasizes the covariances of returns among stock prices irrespective of industry groupings. Therefore a knowledge of the risk/return behavior of stock prices grouped by financial ratios is important in portfolio diversification programs. It may turn out that the returns of two stocks of companies in the same industry have low covariances because of their different financial characteristics. For example, there may be greater difference between stock price changes of Ford and American Motors, even though in the same industry, than there is

---

[a] An "efficient" portfolio is defined as one in which no other mixture of common stocks can give a higher expected return at an equal or lesser expected risk.

between Ford and General Electric because the latter two are more equal in size.

Investment Theory versus Investment Practice

The fifth supporting problem concerns the gap between investment theory and investment practice. Most academicians support the theory that the price of a stock should equal the risk-adjusted present value of some combination of its future dividends, earnings, and terminal market value. On the other hand, a recent survey of practitioners indicates that only about 6 percent of the practitioners calculates present values and that the large majority of them uses some form of financial ratios based on growth, price-earnings ratios, and future return, that is, dividends plus capital gain.[10] Therefore it appears that a gap exists between the approach used by the practitioner and that theorized by the academician. This gap can be narrowed by more research on the nature of security prices and how they respond to different financial measures commonly used by the practitioner and academician.

Understanding Stock Price Behavior as an Aid in Allocating Economic Resources

Finally, and perhaps most important from an economist's viewpoint, research undertaken to more fully understand the nature of common stock prices is critical to the allocation of economic resources. First, stock prices provide information on the company's cost of capital and, therefore, the appropriate level of capital expenditures. Traditionally, a high price-earnings ratio indicates a low cost of equity capital and a demand by investors for a high rate of return on future investment projects. Second, a fair evaluation of an equity provides unbiased information when that company is seeking outside financing. And third, financial analysts influence the flow of funds into those companies considered most undervalued. As pointed out by William J. Baumol: "In sum, the prices assigned to stocks by the free market are critical to the effectiveness of the market as a resource allocator."[11]

Research Methods

In recent years the "black box" approach has gained acceptance as a method of problem solving. The advantage of using the black box approach is that it is not necessary to know the transformation process per se but only what actually takes place. As defined by VanCourt Hare, Jr., "If the input-output relationship observed is sufficiently stable to offer reliable prediction, then that reliable relationship is taken as the black box transformation."[12] As implied in the title of this study, *Financial Ratios and Investment Results*, the inputs are various financial ratios and the outputs are quantitative measures of risk and return from common stocks. It is the relation between these two factors which is examined and not the transformation process itself.

To become involved in the transformation process would require an analysis of the market psychology of investors, a subject beyond the scope of this study. As previously stated, the value of this study lies in presenting the empirical relation between certain financial measures or ratios commonly used in security analysis and risk-adjusted returns from common stocks. Attempts are made at deducing cause-and-effect relationships, for example, low price-earnings ratios generate more risk because they generally have inferior growth, but these deductions are one step removed from the original purpose of the study.

In addition, other research techniques, including interviews, deductive reasoning, statistical methods, and historical analysis based on published and unpublished materials, are used.

Format

The remaining chapters in this study are organized as follows.

Chapter 2 presents the technical and conceptual considerations of the measurement technique used in this study to evaluate risk and return. It focuses on three relevant statistics: first, both the Beta statistic (which measures market or nondiversifiable risk) and the standard error (which measures unique or diversifiable risk) are used to evaluate risk; second, the return is computed as the percentage appreciation, including both dividends and capital changes; and, third, the Alpha statistic, Treynor Index, Sharpe Index, and the Down-Market Index are shown as indicators of risk-adjusted performance.

Chapter 3 describes the ratios to be tested, the input data, the computer output, edit runs, and other factors concerning the methodology and limitations of the study.

Chapter 4 presents evidence on the relation between price-earnings ratios and risk-adjusted returns from common stocks. Some investors prefer stocks with a high price-earnings ratio; others prefer stocks having a low price-earnings ratio. Proponents of the former strategy argue that this ratio is indicative of investor enthusiasm and growth, thereby favoring returns in the form of capital gains. Proponents of the latter strategy argue that low P/E stock is favorable because earnings bought per share of stock not only represent greater value but also these stocks contain less risk.

Chapter 5 looks at the risk-adjusted returns of equities in companies having varying values of one- and four-year earnings growth. Proponents of the growth-stock strategy argue that a company which has reported relatively high earnings growth should be purchased even though its stock may command a high price-earnings ratio as a premium. If the price-earnings ratio does not decline, they argue, the percentage change of the stock will equal or exceed its percentage growth in earnings per share. These growth-stock strategists then are "price-indifferent." In contrast, opponents of this growth-stock strategy argue that the premium is usually too high by the time the earnings are reported and that earnings momentum is not necessarily assured. They conclude that growth stocks generally should be avoided unless the investor has perfect knowledge of the future earnings growth of the company.

Chapter 6 combines the P/E ratio discussed in Chapter 4 and earnings growth strategy in Chapter 5 to identify those securities which may be under- or overvalued, depending on the difference between a theoretical P/E ratio and the actual P/E ratio. As discussed in this chapter, the theoretical P/E ratio according to Graham et al. should approximate 8.5 for zero growth and two more for each 1 percent increase in the earnings growth rate. The risk-adjusted returns are presented for each group of stocks ranked by the amount of this under- or overvaluation.

Chapter 7 presents empirical evidence on the relation between dividend yields and risk-adjusted returns from common stocks. Many investors associate high-yielding stocks with safety of principal; in contrast, low-yielding stocks are sometimes associated with higher probability of capital gains. Therefore a tradeoff appears to exist between yield and capital gain.

Chapter 8 considers the risk/return aspects of stocks of companies having different payout ratios. Graham et al. have stated that

studies made by various analysts—including ourselves—have led to the somewhat surprising conclusion that for typical groups of stocks the weight in the market price of $1 of distributed earnings tended to be about four times as great as that of $1 of retained earnings.[13]

This conclusion should be reexamined, particularly with regard to the effects of risk. Perhaps the stocks of companies which distribute their earnings are only one-fourth as risky as those which retain their earnings.

Chapter 9 looks at the relation between dividend changes and risk-adjusted returns from common stocks. The mathematics in normative models which equate stock prices to the present values of their dividend streams suggest that dividend increases should generate higher equity values, and vice versa. But while most investors would view dividend increases as favorable, others would argue that past dividend increases have already been recognized in the price of the stock.

Chapter 10 examines the relation between total invested capital and risk-adjusted returns. Most investors associate the stocks of companies having large amounts of total invested capital with less risk and lower returns. But do common stocks of larger firms, in fact, exhibit superior risk-adjusted rates of return compared to those of smaller firms?

Chapter 11 presents evidence on the relation between a company's rate of return on total invested capital and its risk-adjusted return from its common stock. The rate of return is sometimes used to reflect how well management is using the financial resources provided to it by its stockholders and creditors. While some investors may feel that a high rate of return is indicative of higher stock prices and less risk, random walkers argue that this historic rate of return is unrelated to future stock prices.

Chapter 12 presents evidence on the risk/return relation between the debt/capital ratio and returns from common stocks. One view is that capital structure does not affect market valuation; the other view is that debt affords an opportunity for earnings leverage and higher market valuation. The traditional view is that there is an optimum amount of debt which results in both a tax advantage and an increase in total company value. But what is the actual experience of stocks of companies which are highly leveraged compared to those which have little or no debt? Does the risk incurred by additional debt flow through to the shareholder in terms of volatility of returns?

Chapter 13 restates the empirical results of the study in three dimensions, namely: (1) risk (Beta), (2) return, and (3) risk-adjusted return (Alpha).

Chapter 14, drawing on the evidence presented in the previous chapters, presents the principle of strategy before selection in portfolio management. This concept suggests that the first question to ask in selecting a particular stock for inclusion in a portfolio is "Which strategy or type of stock?"; the second question is "Which stock?"

Finally, Chapter 15 reviews the entire study to see how the empirical results are related to the hypothesis and other supporting issues.[b]

---

[b]Readers who are familiar with Beta theory and who are not interested in the details of the methodology may turn directly to Chapter 4.

2 Measuring Risk and Risk-adjusted Returns

The initial impetus in developing a quantitative relationship between risk and return came from Harry Markowitz in the mid-1950s, resulting in the publication of his book, *Portfolio Selection: Efficient Diversification of Investments.*[1] Through his efforts, a "theory" of portfolio selection evolved; namely, that under rational decision-making an investor seeks an efficiently diversified portfolio, one in which no other mixture of securities can give a higher expected return at an equal or lesser expected risk. Markowitz attacked the problem through extensive use of quadratic programming in which risks were measured by the variability of returns, and returns were measured by summing capital appreciation and dividends. By combining these measures of risk and return, Markowitz found that efficient portfolios could be generated through proper selection of securities, depending upon the covariances of returns of the individual securities.

Markowitz's theory of portfolio selection took on new dimensions in the 1960s as evidenced by the works of William Sharpe.[2] Sharpe's contribution was to simplify Markowitz's analysis by correlating returns to a single market index. Sharpe found, for example, that an efficient portfolio selected from a list of 100 securities could be generated from 302 input items which link a security's return to the market; in contrast, Markowitz's model required 5150 input items of which 4950 were covariances for each security against every other security. Sharpe's simplification pointed the way to the use of the Alpha and Beta statistics, described later, as indicators of (respectively) risk-adjusted returns and market or nondiversifiable risk. By combining the initial works of Markowitz with the subsequent simplification by Sharpe, one can think of this first phase of risk/return analysis as the *normative* phase since its emphasis was on *how* to construct a portfolio.

Using the Markowitz-Sharpe framework developed in the first phase, Jack Treynor[3] applied these newly developed concepts in the second phase to analyze the performance of mutual funds. Treynor examined the performance of fifty-seven open-end mutual funds using a composite measure of performance involving both risk and return (described later). Using these measures, Treynor found "no evidence to support the belief that mutual fund managers can outguess the market."[4]

In the latter half of the 1960s, the use of Alpha and Beta to measure the performance of pension funds and pension fund managers gained acceptance. This acceptance signaled a shift in emphasis from the original work of Markowitz and Sharpe who concentrated on *how* an investor should select securities, that is, normative decision-making, to one on *how well* portfolio managers have performed. Pension fund managers were subjected to these rigorous measurements to find out if they were, in fact, achieving a return commensurate with the risks they were taking in a particular account.

It is now time to advance this thinking into a third phase, namely, security analysis. It is proposed in this study that the very same theory and statistics used in portfolio selection (phase I) and performance measurement (phase II) be extended to research various hypotheses in security analysis. In effect, one may think of this use as a portfolio selection or performance measurement problem in which "portfolios" are generated based on the value of one or more financial ratios.[a]

Components of Return

Consider a portfolio comprised of a representative sample of the entire market, completely diversified and weighted properly such that a 1 percent increase in the portfolio corresponds exactly to a 1 percent increase in the market. Since this portfolio would increase or decrease as the entire market increased or decreased, the risk of this portfolio is also that of the entire market, and it has a Beta of 1.00 (see Figure 2-1). An investor can increase or decrease his total market risk by varying the proportions of his investments between risk-free assets, which are invariant to the market and his investments in the market. Now consider a portfolio in which the return is 100 percent correlated with the market, but is twice as volatile. If the market increases 1 percent, the portfolio increases 2 percent; if the market decreases 2 percent, the portfolio decreases 4 percent. Such a portfolio has a Beta of 2.0, and has a relatively high market risk (see Figure 2-2). Similarly, if a portfolio were composed of only risk-free assets, its Beta would be zero, since the fluctuations of the portfolio's returns would be invariant to changes in the market (see Figure 2-3).

Now consider portfolio returns which are not highly related with those of the market, as in Figure 2-4.

This portfolio fluctuates somewhat with the market but does not have the same dependence on the market as that shown in the previous figures. Accordingly, in the terminology of this study, the portfolio is not completely diversified and therefore contains relatively more "unique" risk.

---

[a]In this study, the term *portfolio* will be used to mean a group of twenty-five stocks which are "bought" based on the value of one or more financial measures. It is "simulated" in the sense that it reflects what would have happened if an investor had actually made these purchases.

Each of the components illustrated above can be described algebraically. From the aforementioned single index model, the total return of a particular portfolio or security is a function of (1) excess return, (2) a market-risk factor, (3) the market return and (4) a component unique to that particular portfolio or security. Symbolically:

$$R_p = A + BR_m + C$$

where: R_p = return of the portfolio, including capital appreciation plus dividends.

A = Alpha, the Y-intercept; excess return, if there is no change in the market.

B = Beta, the slope of the line when portfolio returns are regressed against market returns; an indicator of market or nondiversifiable risk.

R_m = return of the market, including capital appreciation plus dividends.

C = residual, the variability of which is a measure of unique or diversifiable risk; the expected value of this residual is zero.

In a well-diversified portfolio the most important elements in the analysis are the Alpha and Beta statistics as indicators of risk-adjusted return and market risk. The C component becomes less important for as the number of securities increases, the residuals (C) tend to approach zero. That is, if Alpha and Beta are reliable statistics for large groups of stocks, then the residuals (C) of the returns of each individual security tend to cancel out, thereby minimizing the importance of these residuals in computing returns of a portfolio.

In the case of individual securities, the Alpha and Beta statistics are important only to the degree that the returns of the security are correlated to the least-squares line as security returns are regressed against market returns. If returns are highly correlated, the investment decision is dependent upon the market forecast; if not highly correlated, the investment decision rests upon the unique characteristics of the individual firm. And in this latter case, the C component could dominate the investment decision.

The same reasoning holds true in this study when generating portfolios based on the value of one or more financial ratios. If the standard error of the residuals is relatively high, the confidence one has in that particular financial measure to generate a diversified portfolio is relatively low, and vice versa. An example of this phenomenon is the high price-earnings ratio; in this case the standard error of the residuals of groups of twenty-five high

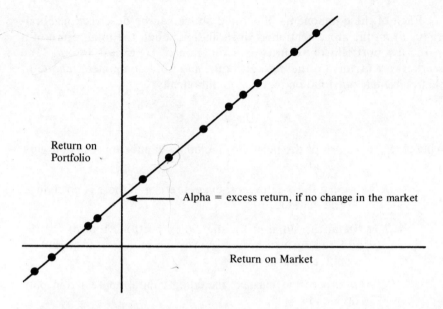

Return on
Portfolio

Alpha = excess return, if no change in the market

Return on Market

Figure 2-1. Beta = 1.00, Alpha = 4.0%, R-Squared = 100%, Standard
Error = 0

P/E stocks was relatively high, thereby indicating that an investor should
be more concerned with the individual stocks comprising the portfolio and
less concerned with overall market movements.

In summary, in measuring the performance of a well-diversified portfolio, that is, in Levy's analysis,[5] perhaps twenty-five stocks or more, and
in certain individual securities which have relatively low standard errors,
the Alpha and Beta statistics along with the overall market movement are
the most important components.

More on The Alpha Statistic

In the prior discussion, Alpha had been defined as the Y-intercept when
returns from a particular portfolio or security are regressed against a
market index. But the interpretation of this Y-intercept is far from clear. A
recent article in a section entitled "Agonizing Over Alpha" in the
Institutional Investor stated:

The alpha factor has yet to be defined with any precision, either theoretically or
empirically. According to most calculations, less than half, and perhaps only a
third, of the fluctuations of the typical stock's rate of return can be explained by its
beta.

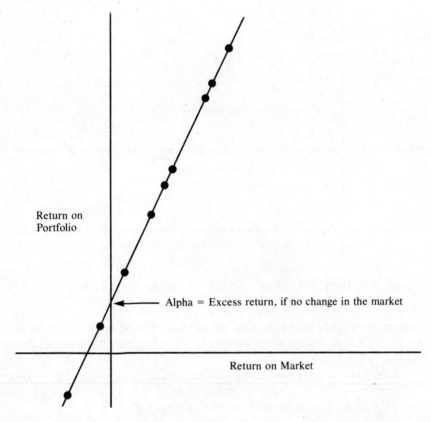

Return on
Portfolio

Alpha = Excess return, if no change in the market

Return on Market

Figure 2-2. Beta = 2.0, Alpha = 4.0%, R-Squared = 100%, Standard Error
= 0

The remainder is due to alpha, and no one knows just how alpha interacts with or
what influence it has on beta.[6]

It is this interaction between Alpha and Beta which causes the most
concern in using Alpha as the sole measure of a portfolio's risk-adjusted
return.

The use of Alpha as a statistical measure of performance was explained
by Michael Jensen:

Thus if the portfolio manager has an ability to forecast security prices, the intercept
[Alpha] . . . will be positive. Indeed, it represents the average incremental rate of
return on the portfolio per unit time which is due solely to the manager's ability to
forecast future security prices. It is interesting to note that a naive random selection
buy and hold policy can be expected to yield a zero intercept. In addition if the
manager is not doing as well as a random selection buy and hold policy [Alpha] will
be negative.[7]

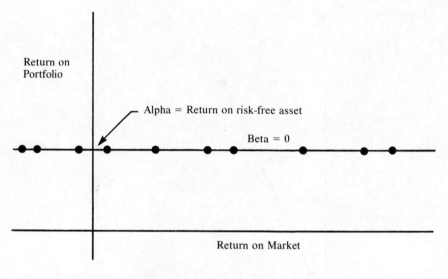

Figure 2-3. Beta = 0, Alpha = 4.0%, Standard Error = 0

Jensen then adds that the standard error of estimate of Alpha is also necessary to judge whether or not the particular value of Alpha was due to chance rather than skill.

Jensen also argues that Alpha has the advantage of measuring absolute performance as well as relative performance. The reason for this is that Jensen's Alpha is calculated from the expression:

$$R_p - r^* = A + B(R_m - r^*) + C$$

where: R_p = return of the portfolio.

r^* = risk-free rate of return.

A = Alpha, the Y-intercept.

B = Beta, the slope of the line regressing portfolio returns against market returns.

R_m = return of the market.

C = residual; expected value = 0.

Note that this model is very similar to the single-index model previously discussed, but that a risk-free rate of return is included. It is this inclusion which transforms Alpha into an absolute measure of performance for it indicates how well a portfolio has done over and above a risk-free investment in (say) treasury bills.

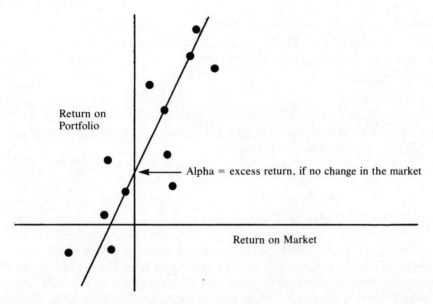

Return on
Portfolio

Alpha = excess return, if no change in the market

Return on Market

Figure 2-4. Beta = 2.0, Alpha = 4.0%, R-Squared = 70%, Standard Error
= 5.0

While intuitively appealing, Alpha as a measure of investment performance has been challenged. Subsequent to Jensen's work, further studies on price changes of individual stocks indicate that those with a low Beta tend to have a high Alpha, and those with a high Beta tend to have a low Alpha.[8] It is this concept that caused the aforementioned Chris Welles to observe: "no one knows just how alpha interacts with or what influence it has on beta." That is, Jensen assumes independence, other studies show dependence. If the Alpha versus Beta relationship found for individual stocks is also present for portfolios, then there will be a tendency for conservative portfolios with a low Beta to outperform the more volatile, high-Beta portfolios since, as a group, they will tend to have higher Alphas.

The Alpha statistic, however, would be important in measuring the performance of portfolios in the same risk class, that is, portfolios with approximately equal Betas. This concept is shown graphically in Figure 2-5. Clearly, portfolio A has superior performance compared to that of portfolio B for the rate of return of portfolio A always exceeds that of B irrespective of the change in the overall market. In this case, the Alpha statistic would be a satisfactory measure to rank performance.

Other One-Parameter Measures

At least two authors, namely, William F. Sharpe[9] and Jack L. Treynor,[10] have developed measures which combine risk and return into one composite measure. First, Sharpe defined his measure as follows:

$$SI = \frac{R_p - r^*}{s}$$

where: SI = Sharpe Index; the excess return per unit of ex post risk, or the reward to risk ratio.

R_p = return of the portfolio.

r^* = risk-free return.

s = standard deviation of returns.

Second, Treynor developed a composite index of performance very similar to Sharpe's index, the major difference being that Treynor separates risk into its component parts, nondiversifiable (market) risk and residual (nonmarket) risk. While Sharpe ranks performance using total variability in the denominator of his composite measure, Treynor includes only nondiversifiable (market) risk.

Treynor's formula is:[b]

$$TI = \frac{R_p - r^*}{B}$$

where: TI = Treynor Index; the excess return per unit of ex post nondiversifiable risk, or the reward to risk ratio.

R_p = return of the portfolio.

r^* = risk-free return.

B = Beta, a measure of nondiversifiable (market) risk.

In discussing the advantages of using the standard deviation in the denominator rather than Treynor's Beta, Sharpe explains:

The Treynor Index cannot capture the portion of variability that is due to lack of

---

[b]Treynor than adds another composite measure which is consistent with the first:

$$TI = \frac{r^* - A}{B}$$

Where A is the intercept of the regression line at the point where market yield equals zero. In contrast to Treynor's first measure, the lower the value of TI, the better the performance of the portfolio.

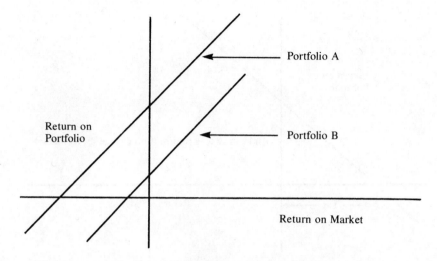

Figure 2-5. Equal Betas; Unequal Alphas

diversification. For this reason it is an inferior measure of *past* performance. But for this reason it may be a superior measure for predicting *future* performance.[11]

Sharpe then shows empirically that both measures give very similar rankings.

Another distinction between the Beta and the variance is argued by Friend et al.

The Beta coefficient might be considered more applicable for an investor in a mutual fund with other fund or stock investments, while the variance measure is more applicable to an investor in a mutual fund with no other investments in securities.[12]

From an operative viewpoint, the Beta statistic has the advantage of providing a technique to integrate market forecasts with security selection. For example, the Beta approach implies that high Beta stocks should be purchased if the market forecast is positive and, alternatively, that low or negative Beta stocks should be purchased if a market decline is forecast. In this study, if a rise in the market is forecast, an investor should purchase the stock of companies exhibiting financial ratios consistent with high Betas; alternatively, in market declines an investor—if required to hold equities—should hold stocks of companies exhibiting financial ratios associated with low Betas.

Another measure which has intuitive appeal and is highly correlated with both the Sharpe Index and the Treynor Index is:

$$DR = - \frac{A}{B}$$

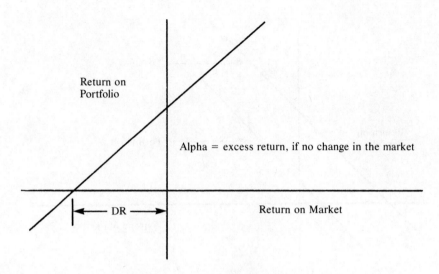

Return on
Portfolio

Alpha = excess return, if no change in the market

DR

Return on Market

Figure 2-6. *DR* as a Measure of Risk

where: *DR* = downside risk of the overall market.

      A = Alpha, the *Y*-intercept.

      B = Beta, the slope of the line regressing portfolio returns against market returns.

The measure DR, as seen in Figure 2-6, reflects the amount that the market must decline before a well-diversified portfolio will show a loss. It is, in fact, Treynor's modified index without the risk-free rate. For example, a portfolio with an Alpha of 4.0 and a Beta of 0.5 would show a gain as long as the market did not change by more than −4.0/0.5, or −8 percent.

The One-Parameter Problem

The basic issue here, however, is whether or not a ratio which includes return in the numerator and some measure of volatility (either Beta or the standard deviation) in the denominator does in fact measure investment performance. The concept to be reflected in this ratio is that investors prefer maximum returns at minimum risk. Therefore the higher this ratio, that is, return per unit of risk, the better the performance.

    One problem that may arise is that as volatility or risk approaches zero, the ratio approaches infinity. As a result, portfolios which are practically risk-free but yield only a slight return over and above the risk-free rate will show exaggerated performance. For example, if the yield on sixty-day Treasury Bills is defined as the risk-free return, the performance rating of an investment in (say) a slightly higher yielding ninety-day Treasury Bill, which has a Beta and standard deviation close to zero, would be near infinity. But certainly such a rating should not imply "infinity" performance.

The same argument prevails as one progresses to the slightly more volatile utility stocks, then bank stocks, and so forth, perhaps to the most volatile new issue market. In the new issue market, for example, one could show an exceptionally high return but the measure of risk may be so high that the composite measure would actually show inferior performance. In this case one could triple the value of his investment while continuing to show an inferior performance.

The problem here is that risk and return are not necessarily linearly related if extreme values are considered. In such cases these measures are highly suspect, and the predominant factor becomes return, relegating risk to a more subjective, less quantifiable, role.

Summary

Measuring risk and return, has been a subject gaining more and more acceptance. While originally developed by Markowitz as a normative tool for constructing efficient portfolios, it later became a technique for measuring the performance of portfolio managers and mutual funds. It is now proposed in this study to use this technique in security analysis to identify the risks and returns associated with a particular financial ratio.

Now let us turn to the next chapter, which describes the procedures and data used in this study to find the actual (ex post) relation between risk-adjusted returns from common stocks and some financial ratios.

3 Design of the Experiment

The first paragraph in Chapter 1 stated this study's hypothesis to be "that certain commonly used financial measures or ratios generally known to the financial community have no inherent value in determining risk-adjusted returns from common stocks. This hypothesis, if true, suggests that stock prices are determined only by future events, thereby supporting both the broad form of the random-walk hypothesis and its related efficiency of the marketplace."

The task of this chapter is to describe the experiment used to draw conclusions regarding the validity of this hypothesis.

Selecting the Measures to be Tested

The commonly used financial measures or ratios examined in this study include:

1. Price-earnings (P/E) ratio
2. Growth in earnings per share
3. P/E relative to earnings growth
4. Dividend yield
5. Changes in dividends per share
6. Payout ratio
7. Total invested capital
8. Rate of return
9. Debt/capital ratio

These measures were selected by the author after discussion with various practicing investment analysts. In addition, it appears that these measures are among those most frequently used in textbooks on security analysis. But by no means is this select list of ratios meant to be all-inclusive.

Note that each measure by itself has an innumerable number of variations. For example, in testing the relation between the price-earnings ratio, growth rate and stock price changes, should one use prior year's earnings in the denominator or some form of normalized earnings? Should the closing price of the stock be used in the numerator or should the average of the high and low price for the year be used? In computing growth rates, what time period should be used to reflect growth? Should an average, compound or least-squares growth rate be computed? And most important, what mathematical relationship should be used in equating growth rates to price-earnings ratios? Additional complications arise when contemplating the numerous combinations of measures which can be tested. For example, one may rank ratios first by the P/E ratio of the stock and second by the growth rate of the company within P/E groups.

Because only a few measures and a few variations within each measure are being tested, the broad form of the random-walk hypothesis would not necessarily be proven even if the evidence indicated no relation. The reason for this lack of proof is that other measures not yet tested may result in opposite conclusions. In contrast, if a significant relation does exist for one or more of the ratios, then the broad form of the random-walk hypothesis would be disproven.

Choosing a Standard of Comparison

Chapter 2 discussed measures of risk, both market (nondiversifiable) risk and unique (diversifiable) risk. The point was made that in a well-diversified portfolio, market risk can be measured by its Beta, the slope of the line when portfolio returns are regressed against the returns of the "general market."

The question then becomes, what is the proper measure of the "general market" when calculating this Beta? The immediate reaction to this question is to respond with the widely used Dow Jones or Standard & Poor's 425 Indexes. Upon closer examination, however, each of these indexes has certain defaults. The Dow Jones, for example, is (1) limited to only thirty stocks, (2) biased toward high-priced issues so that a stock selling at $100 has twice the weight as that of a stock priced at $50, and (3) unequal in its treatment of stock splits and stock dividends; for example, if a stock splits two for one, it has only half the weight in the averages that it previously had.

The broader Standard & Poor's 425 is a satisfactory measure of the general market of industrial prices in terms of total dollars because each stock price is weighted by the number of shares outstanding. However, this advantage is also a disadvantage for purposes of this study because the focus of attention here is on the *individual* (unweighted) issue. That is, since this study analyzes the performance of individual issues, performance must be compared to that of the average individual issue. And this performance of the average individual issue may or may not be closely correlated to that of a weighted index, depending on the relation of stock price returns of large companies vis-à-vis small companies.

Because of this incomparability, a new index was developed for purposes of this study. This new index is computed as the average unweighted percentage change of all stocks in the S & P 425. As such, it is assumed that equal dollars are invested in the shares of each company to be tested. This approach is also more consistent with that used by the average investor. Levy points out that

although the Standard & Poor's indices may be representative of the holdings of all investors combined, they are not typical of the average investor. The average investor is much more likely to buy either an equal number of shares of the stocks he selects (as assumed by the Dow-Jones averages) or an equal number of dollars worth. . . . He would not likely weight his investment in individual securities by their aggregate market values.[1]

This new unweighted index then is simply:

$$R_m = \frac{\sum_1^N [(P_t - P_{t-1})/P_{t-1} + D]}{N}$$

where: R_m = return of the market.

N = number of stocks, i.e., 425, except where data were not available.

P = price of the stock.

D = dividend return.

This average percentage return, R_m, calculated from the above equation is used as the independent variable in computing the risk/return measures discussed in Chapter 2.

Choosing a Methodology

Regression analysis has been widely used by statisticians and market analysts in "explaining" stock prices. But in contrast to this study which uses the general market (R_m) as the independent variable, the more direct method is to use earnings, dividends, book value, cash flow, and other fundamental and/or technical data as the independent variable. Perhaps the earliest reported attempt to use this more direct approach was in 1935, when J.W. Meader published his paper on "A Formula for Determining

Basic Values Underlying Common Stock Price.''[2] His regression using 502 stocks on the NYSE for the year 1933 was as follows:

$$P = 1.7 + 1.35S + 0.12B + 0.20W + 3.0E + 8.40D$$

where: P = mean price of the stock in 1933.

   S = turnover (shares traded).

   B = book value per share.

   W = net working capital per share.

   E = earnings per share.

   D = dividends per share.

These equations were computed from time to time by Meader until it became clear to him that the coefficients were not too stable. After ten years of studying these equations, Meader states:

If any general conclusion can be drawn from this 10-year series of multiple correlation studies, it is a negative one. The assumption that current dividends and earnings, among other bits of arithmetic, are acceptable criteria of investment value when tested quantitatively by market prices over an extended period did not yield close or consistent results.[3]

Similarly, *The Value Line Investment Survey* has used both fundamental and technical data as independent variables in their regression equations.[4] However, in contrast to Meader's approach which regressed data on many companies for each year, Value Line regressed the data on individual companies over several years. For example, in ranking the stock of General Motors for probable market performance in the next twelve months, Value Line derived the formula:[5]

$$P = -13.39 + 1.42B + 3.56D + 4.00E + 0.23P$$

where: P = estimated price.

   B = book value per share.

   D = dividends per share.

   E = earnings per share.

   P = prior year's price.

Until revised in 1965, Value Line had several problems in using this regression method: (1) the computations did not easily reflect the relative valuation of a particular stock compared to all other stocks; (2) the number of observations for each company were too few; (3) the independent variables were highly interdependent; and, most important, (4) accurate estimates were required for earnings, dividends, and book value.

In 1965 Value Line discontinued this time-series regression method in favor of one which used only historical data, thereby eliminating the need for accurate estimates. This newer technique involved three independent variables, (1) a comparison of recent earnings and prices with the earnings and prices for the prior ten years, (2) a comparison of the average P/E ratio with the average five year P/E ratio, and (3) the earnings momentum of the company on a quarter to quarter basis. The values of these three factors are summed and ranked so that the highest ranked stocks become those most likely to outperform the remaining stocks over the next twelve months.

These two examples, Meader's and Value Line's, are typical of the regression approach using fundamental and/or technical data as the independent variable. While the former was skeptical about this approach, the latter has had apparent success.[6] But the question remaining in the Value Line approach is the treatment of risk and the interdependency of the independent variables. Indeed, while the Value Line approach casts doubt on the validity of the broad form of the random-walk hypothesis, more study is needed on the concept of risk-adjusted returns. For example, if Alpha/Beta measures are used, what is the relation between the ratios used by Value Line and investment results?

In this context, the use of returns from the general market (R_m) instead of fundamental and/or technical data as the independent variable provides an added dimension to some of the work in security analysis already undertaken. First, regressions against the general market permit an Alpha/Beta type of analysis commonly used in portfolio theory and portfolio measurement. Second, the use of one variable at a time avoids the interdependency problem normally found in regression equations. Therefore, primarily for these two reasons, the Alpha/Beta methodology was chosen.

Justification for a Twenty-five Stock Portfolio

In this study, portfolios containing 25 stocks each are generated from a universe of 425 stocks. The criterion for inclusion is the value of one or more financial ratios. The question here is whether or not a 25-stock portfolio is sufficient.

Adequate diversification can be obtained from using relatively few stocks in a portfolio. For example, H.A. Latane and W.E. Young showed that little benefit can be derived from diversifying beyond 16 stocks.[7] The returns from stocks chosen at random from a sample of 224 stocks over eighty-five overlapping twelve-month periods from January 1953 to December 1960 were as follows:

No. of Stocks in Portfolio	Compound Return	Percentage of 2.5% Ret. Diff. Eliminated by Additional Diversification
1	1.126	
4	1.144	68
8	1.147	16
16	1.149	8
32	1.150	4
224	1.151	4

As shown above, selecting 4 stocks instead of 1 accounted for about 68 percent of the difference in the return; selecting 8 stocks instead of 4 accounted for 16 percent of the difference; and selecting 32 stocks instead of 16 accounted for only 4 percent of the difference. A study by J.L. Evans and S.H. Archer showed similar results.[8]

In still another study, Jack E. Gaumnitz found that beyond 18 holdings the unique or diversifiable risk was minimal.[9] This study involved the computation of monthly returns for a sample of 140 corporations over the time period 1960 to 1963. A summary of the results expressing risk as a percentage of the risk of a portfolio of 140 stocks is found below:

Number of Holdings	3	6	11	18	26	36	44
Average Risk of 5 Portfolios	126	112	107	105	101	105	107

Based on the results of these studies, the chances of error in using groups of 25 stocks to generate a portfolio from the value of one or more financial ratios are very small.

Choosing a Time Frame or Holding Period

With the increasing emphasis on short-term performance, mutual funds and other financial institutions direct their research efforts toward finding securities which should perform well over a six- to twelve-month period. The rationale behind this approach is twofold; first, analysts find it most difficult to forecast earnings accurately more than one year in advance and, second, since long-term performance evolves from combined short-term performances, an investor maximizes his long-term returns by maximizing his short-term returns. This approach prevailed among many portfolio managers during the 1960s and resulted in a substantial increase in the number of shares traded. However, evidence to date has not confirmed that this approach results in superior investment performance.

In this study the choice of a time frame or holding period is critical for what may be valid during one time frame may not be valid in another. For example, low P/E stocks may offer defensive (low Beta) characteristics over six months but not over one year. Levy's studies on the stationarity of Beta coefficients confirm that the holding period is indeed relevant. He found that "for portfolios of 25 stocks and larger, over forecast intervals of 26 weeks and longer, past risk is an excellent proxy for future risk."[10]

In view of the time-frame problem, three calculations are made in this study: (1) percentage returns over one year using year-end prices, (2) percentage returns over two years using year-end prices, and (3) percentage returns over one year using the average high/low price of the stock. The relevant formulas then in computing these returns are, respectively:

$$\text{Return} = \frac{\text{Ending Price in Year 2} - \text{Ending Price in Year 1} + \text{Dividends}}{\text{Ending Price Year 1}}$$

$$\text{Return} = \frac{\text{Ending Price in Year 3} - \text{Ending Price in Year 1} + \text{Dividends}}{\text{Ending Price in Year 1}}$$

$$\text{Return} = \frac{\text{Average Price in Year 2} - \text{Average Price in Year 1} + \text{Dividends}}{\text{Average Price in Year 1}}$$

There are at least two reasons for calculating returns using three different pricing intervals. First, sampling errors are minimized in the event that the price of an equity happens to be unrepresentative of its normal price on one particular day. Second, the more time periods used, the more assurance one has in the results. In any respect, intuition suggests that if a link does exist between financial ratios and investment results, this link should be invariant with time, whether it be one year, two years, or an "average" year. If not invariant, then either the link does, in fact, exist for one period and not for the next or the evidence is subject to suspect. However, as it turns out, the evidence does show surprising consistency, particularly between the one- and two-year periods using year-end prices.

Input Data

The data base used in this study was compiled by Investment Management

Sciences, a division of Standard & Poor's Corporation, and translated by them onto magnetic tape. This tape was purchased by Marine Midland Banks, Inc., which made it available to the author. The entire data base consists of sixty financial measures (including items from the balance sheet and profit-and-loss statement) on about 900 companies over the twenty-year period from 1952 to 1971.

While the entire data base contains information on about 900 major industrial companies, many of these companies were added to the data base only after they achieved a reasonable degree of financial success. Therefore, if all the 900 companies were used in the study this addition would cause a historical bias. To help minimize this historical bias, the following steps were taken:

1. Only companies in the S & P 425 were included. These companies are generally well-recognized firms representing a cross-section of American industry.
2. If the necessary data for a particular ratio were not immediately available in the data base in a particular year, the company was not included in the study. No attempt was made to reconstruct this missing data under the assumption that if the data were not readily available to Standard & Poor, it would not be readily available to the financial community.
3. Companies with sales less than $50 million were excluded. This exclusion avoided the bias of including small companies which were added to the S & P 425 only after they attained reasonable success.

Even after minimizing some of the bias found in the original data base, it is likely that some bias still remains. However, this remaining bias should not materially affect the results of this study.

Computer Output

The following statistics are shown for each of the ranked groups of twenty-five stocks over the entire 20-year period. (See, for example, Tables 4-1, 4-2, and 4-3 in the next chapter):

Return-Group: The average percentage return per year of each group.

Return-All: The average percentage return per year of all stocks, i.e., the market.

Pct Over: The average percentage of the number of stocks in the group which outperformed the market.

Beta:	The slope of the line when *Return-Group* is regressed against *Return-All*, i.e., a measure of nondiversifiable or market risk.
Std Err Beta:	The standard error of Beta, described above; a measure of Beta reliability.
Std Err Alpha	The standard error of Alpha.
R Squared:	The coefficient of determination when *Return-Group* is regressed against *Return-All*, i.e., a measure of how much of the total group fluctuations can be explained by market fluctuations.
T Value:	Beta divided by the standard error of Beta, a test of the relative statistical significance of Beta.
Geom Mean:	The geometric mean of the return of the group based on a unit value of 1.00 in the initial year.
Std Dev Group:	The standard deviation of *Return-Group*.
Std Err Est:	The standard error of estimate when *Return-Group* is regressed against *Return-All*; a measure of how well a portfolio is diversified, i.e., the unique risk.
Alpha:	The Y-intercept when *Return-Group* is regressed against *Return-All*; sometimes referenced as the excess or risk-adjusted return.
Sharpe Index:	The Sharpe Index calculated by dividing the *Return-Group* by the *Std Dev Group*; a composite measure of risk-adjusted performance.
Treynor Index:	The Treynor Index found by dividing the *Return-Group* by *Beta*; a composite measure of risk-adjusted performance.
Down Market Index:	The Down Market Index calculated by dividing *Alpha* by *Beta*; a composite measure of risk-adjusted performance.

A group summary is provided for each of the three time frames (see the earlier section, "Choosing a Time Frame on Holding Period") and for each of the ratios or measures under analysis.

Summary

This chapter described the methodology and data used to show the relation between certain financial measures and the risks and returns from common stocks. The salient points covered in this chapter were as follows:

	Group	Ranking
Top Group	1	1 to 25
	2	26 to 50
	3	51 to 75
Middle Group		Between the end of group 3 and the beginning of group 4
Bottom Group	4	End of middle group, plus 25
	5	End of group 4, plus 25
	6[a]	End of group 5, plus 25

[a]Normally, the last-ranked stock in group 6 would be number 425, the number of stocks in the S & P 425, but data were not available in every year.

1. A few financial measures were selected for analysis. These measures, in this researcher's opinion, are those most frequently studied and used both by security analysts and academics.

2. The popular averages, that is, the Dow Jones and Standard & Poor's Indexes, were found to be unsuitable as a standard of comparison for measuring performance. Accordingly, a revised unweighted index was computed for purposes of this study.

3. While most equity-valuation studies use various "causal" factors such as earnings, dividends, and book value as independent variables in the regression equation, this study uses returns from the market as the independent variable. The main advantage of using market returns instead of "causal" factors as the independent variable is that nondiversifiable and unique risk can be identified in a context consistent with portfolio theory.

4. Evidence was presented that justified the use of twenty-five stocks in a portfolio. Too small a sample would create excessive variability, that is, unique risk, and too large a sample would blur the results.

5. In order to minimize sampling errors, this study used three different pricing periods, that is, over one year using year-end prices; over two years using year-end prices; and over one year using the average high/low price during the year.

6. The input data, purchased by Marine Midland Banks from Investment Management Sciences, Standard & Poor's, Inc., for the author's use, include sixty financial measures on about 900 companies over the period 1952 to 1971. To minimize bias, this data base was condensed to include only companies in the S & P 425 where data were available.

With this in mind, let us now turn to a discussion of each of the financial measures mentioned in this chapter together with some of the findings. First, consider the P/E ratio and investment results.

4 The P/E Ratio and Investment Results

This chapter discusses the nature of the price-earnings (P/E) ratio in security analysis and then presents the results of some empirical tests on the risk/return relation between the P/E ratio and returns from common stocks.

In this respect, two empirical studies are presented. The first study is based on the value of the P/E without regard to the direction of earnings —and therefore has the disadvantage of having nonhomogeneous companies within one particular grouping. (For example, in this first study, a stock having a high P/E caused by an earnings decline would be included in the same group as a stock with a high P/E caused by a price increase. The former may represent a decaying company while the latter may be a growing company. Other reasons for a high P/E may be that the price declined less than the earnings, or the price rose while earnings stayed the same; or the price was the same while earnings declined. In any case, there is a problem in this first study of creating well-defined homogeneous groups based on a single value of the P/E ratio.) The second study eliminates some of this nonhomogeneity by including only those companies which reported an earnings increase. If companies are regrouped in this manner, it is seen that the results are slightly different.

The chapter is divided into three parts; first, the traditional arguments for buying high and low P/E stocks are discussed; second, the results of a few prior studies on the P/E ratio are given; and third, the empirical results of the two aforementioned studies are presented.

The Traditional Approach

In arriving at a P/E for a particular stock, an investor traditionally weighs factors such as the risks involved, the company's dividend policy, its stability of earnings, and its expected growth. If he concludes that the current price-earnings ratio is too low, the stock is considered undervalued; if too high, it is overvalued. In weighing these factors, the investor normally uses a decision process which is largely judgmental and intuitive. This traditional approach follows the general principles of analysis suggested by most authorities.

But is there an unknown bias which may exist among investors in assigning a P/E ratio to a particular stock? The fact that a stock currently sells at a relatively low P/E may suggest to an analyst that the stock is underpriced, or if not underpriced that the future prospects of the company are in doubt. Perhaps some investors intuitively dislike low P/E stocks, even though it may turn out that low P/E stocks as a group are in fact temporarily undervalued, that is, thereby denying the status of the market-place as an efficient allocator of resources.

Consider the following hypotheses regarding high versus low P/E stocks:

1. Low P/E stocks are less risky than high P/E stocks. The rationale here is that a minimum P/E exists such that in a market decline the prices of stocks with a low P/E will not fall as much as those with a high P/E.
2. High P/E stocks are less risky than low P/E stocks. The rationale behind this argument is that a high price-earnings ratio is indicative of investor enthusiasm and growth; as such, they are not risky in the long run for they generally provide high returns in the form of capital appreciation.
3. Low P/E stocks give higher returns than high P/E stocks. The reason for these higher returns is that earnings bought per dollar of low P/E stock are greater than those of high P/E stock. Furthermore, since the growth of a company is difficult to predict, an investor should assign greater weight to current earnings than to future earnings, thereby making low P/E stocks more attractive than high P/E stocks.
4. High P/E stocks give greater total returns to the investor than low P/E stocks. Apparently, in the long run, capital gains received from growth-type, high P/E stocks are usually superior to that received from low P/E stocks. Therefore, it is argued, a portfolio structured toward high P/E stocks is likely to outperform a portfolio containing low P/E stocks.
5. Neither a high P/E nor a low P/E is indicative of future performance on a risk-adjusted basis, a conclusion consistent with the random-walk hypothesis. The argument here is that the marketplace is a highly efficient mechanism in which all information is immediately discounted in the price of the stock. Therefore, on a risk-adjusted basis, the fact that a stock has either a high or a low P/E does not necessarily suggest superior investment performance.

From the above statements, each one seemingly correct in the absence of further evidence, an investor cannot deduce any one consistent principle which may be useful to him in his investment decision.

Prior Studies on the P/E Ratio

S. Francis Nicholson

Nicholson studied the returns of 100 common stocks over varying time spans from 1939 to 1959 and found that the 20 lowest P/E stocks showed more appreciation than the 20 highest.[1] The middle groups generally appreciated less than the 20 lowest P/E stocks, but oftentimes this middle group also appreciated less than the 20 highest P/E stocks. In a similar study involving 29 chemical companies, Nicholson found that the lowest P/E stocks appreciated more than the highest P/E stocks in more than 80 percent of the number of time periods studied. Based on these two studies, his conclusion was that:

These studies seem to confirm that present or immediately prospective earnings are a major factor in the outlook for market prices of common stocks. Many investors have apparently underestimated the importance of reasonable price-earnings relationships.

High price-earnings multiples typically reflect investor satisfaction with companies of high quality, or with those which have experienced several years of expansion and rising earnings. In such cases, prices have risen faster than earnings. . . . When this occurs, upward price trends are eventually subject to slowdown or reversal.[2]

Another study by Nicholson reaffirmed his previous findings that low P/E stock offers greater rewards on the average than high P/E stock.[3] This study involved the performance of the stocks of 189 companies in eighteen industries over the period 1937 to 1962. The results of his tests again showed that the lowest P/E stocks, grouped according to quintiles, outperformed the highest P/E stocks:

Grouped by Quintile	Average Percentage of Change After One Year
Lowest P/E	16%
Next higher	9
Next higher	7
Next higher	6
Highest P/E	3

In summary, both studies by Nicholson show that low P/E stocks should be preferred over high or middle P/E stocks.

James D. McWilliams

McWilliams studied the effect of the price-earnings ratio on the returns of 390 stocks over the period 1953 to 1964.[4] His results were consistent with those reported by Nicholson, that is, favoring low P/E stocks:

The study shows that better investment performance can be obtained from a portfolio comprised of low price-earnings ratio stocks as contrasted to portfolios made up of high price-earnings ratio stocks.[5]

Unlike the Nicholson study, however, McWilliams computed the standard deviation of returns for each decile in the 390-stock sample and found that the first decile of low P/E stocks showed as much variability, that is, total risk, as the tenth decile which contained the high P/E stocks. The middle group exhibited less variability than either the highest or lowest P/E group. He concluded that an investor would improve performance by buying low P/E stocks, perhaps in the third and fourth decile, and consider the first decile of low P/E stocks only relative to the additional risks involved. With regard to professional portfolio management, McWilliams observed that most institutions usually weight their portfolios with stocks in the seventh, eighth, and ninth deciles, a group which has not performed particularly well.

McWilliams also concluded that there is no relation between *number* of stocks exhibiting superior performance and the price-earnings ratio. Stocks which had the highest appreciation were found in equal numbers in each P/E decile. However, the number of stocks which showed the greatest declines were generally found in the high P/E groups.

Paul F. Miller and Ernest R. Widman

Miller and Widman of Drexel Harriman Ripley Incorporated, examined the price performance of low P/E versus high P/E industrial stocks for the period 1948 to 1964. The number of companies in the study varied from 110 in 1948 to 334 in 1964 and included only those which had (1) annual sales exceeding $150 million, (2) positive earnings and (3) a fiscal year ending between September 30 and January 31. Homogeneous groups were obtained each year by dividing the entire group into quintiles, and the average return of each quintile was then calculated by dividing the total return from year to year by the number of stocks.

Again, as in both the Nicholson and the McWilliams study, the results of the study indicated that

The low price-earnings group has consistently outperformed the high price-earnings group. In fact, there is a distinct tendency for the groups to fall in a pattern of inverse rank correlation with the height of the P/E ratio.[6]

In another study by the Drexel firm, the stocks in the Dow Jones Industrial Average were divided into three equal groups of low P/E, middle P/E, and high P/E multiples. Using a periodic reinvestment plan whereby the ten highest P/E stocks would be purchased each year, a $10,000 investment in June 1936 would have appreciated to $25,347 by June 1962; the same investment in middle P/E ratio stock would have grown to $43,672; and, in comparison, the $10,000 invested in low P/E stock would have appreciated to $66,866. Note that in this study the survival bias is minimized. Whereas previous studies could be criticized for including low P/E stocks which survived to later become high P/E stocks, this study comprises only stocks of companies in the Dow Jones Average—a group well-defined in a historic context.

William Breen

Breen confirmed the conclusions of Nicholson, McWilliams, and Miller on the superior performance of low P/E stocks but used a measuring technique and sample selection procedure that was more refined than earlier studies on this subject.[7] First, with regard to the measuring technique, Breen compared the returns of low P/E stocks to randomly generated portfolios consisting of the same number of stocks as in the low P/E group. For example, he compared the performance of a group of ten low P/E stocks against a group of ten randomly selected stocks; and a group of fifty low P/E stocks against a group of fifty stocks selected at random. This technique eliminated much of the bias caused by either a weighted market index such as the Standard and Poor's 500 or an unweighted index such as the Dow Jones Average, which is overly sensitive to high-priced issues.

Second, Breen excluded from his sample all companies that failed to maintain a 10 percent growth rate over the prior five-year period. Because of this exclusion, one may question whether Breen's analysis showed the (1) superior results from low P/E stocks, (2) inferior results from non-growth stocks, or (3) both. Breen's own conclusion favors the low P/E variable as the dominant one while relegating growth to the status of a control variable. More on this issue will be found in Chapter 5.

Third, in contrast to prior studies, Breen defined a low P/E as one being low relative to both the market as well as the industry. In this regard, Breen found that decisions based on market relatives instead of industry relatives tended to give superior results:

The evidence seems to (weakly) support the hypothesis that the relevant measure of low price-earnings multiples is a comparison based on the whole market, rather than on an industry basis.[8]

Breen's results are impressive. Over the fourteen-year period, the returns of the ten lowest P/E stocks relative to the market outperformed a random selection of ten stocks 86 percent of the number of times. In only one year, 1957, was this average below 50 percent. On an industry basis, the average number of times that the ten lowest P/E stocks outperformed a random selection was 74 percent. There were three years, (1957, 1962, and 1965) in which this average was below 50 percent. Breen's conclusions were that low price-earnings multiples, measured either relative to the whole population, or to industry classification, when combined with a control on average past growth in earnings, give portfolio performance which in most years is superior to the performance of randomly selected securities.[9]

Frederick Fluegel

Fluegel, in contrast to most researchers, found that the return on high P/E stocks is approximately the same as that for low P/E stocks.[10] He reported that the low P/E stocks selected in the years studied, 1951 to 1955, achieved a rate of return of 11.9 percent while that for high P/E stocks was 10.7 percent, a difference which he rejected at the 0.05 significance level. In measuring return, Fluegel discounted the dividends and ending price over a ten-year period using a 6 percent discount rate and then compared this result to the starting price. These computations were made for both high and low P/E stocks selected at random from *Moody's Handbook of Common Stocks, 1966*. A low P/E was arbitrarily identified as less than 15 and a high P/E as greater than 20.

Fluegel's methodology, however, is suspect. First, only the period 1951-1955 was tested, a questionable number of data points to prove a hypothesis. Second, only 10 stocks were chosen for each high/low, P/E category, a questionable number of stocks for analysis. Third, the 10 stocks chosen were selected using random numbers and arbitrarily classified as high if the P/E were over 20 or low if under 15; as such many very high or very low P/E's may have been excluded in the sample. (Perhaps a ranking procedure would have been more informative.) Fourth, stocks were chosen without regard to size or exchange listing. Fifth, no differentiation was made between stocks which sold at a high P/E due to an earnings decline rather than a price increase. And, sixth, no adjustment was made for risk. In summary, this study has serious limitations and must be used cautiously in refuting the hypothesis that low P/E stocks and high P/E stocks are two distinct homogeneous groups in terms of risk and return.

Results—The P/E Ratio

In general, almost all prior studies suggest that low P/E stocks give superior investment performance compared to that of high P/E stocks. But more refinement is necessary. How about the effects of risk? What happens if only the companies in the S & P 425 are analyzed? What earnings should be used in the study? But, most important, how should investment results be measured? Let us now consider the results of this study.

The empirical evidence presented in Tables 4-1, 4-2, and 4-3 on P/E ratios[a] and investments results suggest that:

1. *Risk*. Low P/E stocks exhibit more market risk but less unique risk than high P/E stocks.

2. *Return*. Low P/E stocks show higher returns than high P/E stocks when measured over one- and two-year periods. If the high-low average price is used to calculate returns, the higher returns of low P/E stocks is not evident.

3. *Risk-adjusted Results*. On a risk-adjusted, one-parameter basis, the results are somewhat inconclusive but tend to favor high P/E stocks, depending on the time period used. An investment in low P/E stocks over a one-year horizon (Table 4-1) shows mixed performance; over a two-year period (Table 4-2) the performance of the very lowest P/E group appears inferior and the very highest superior; and on an average high/low return basis (Table 4-3), high P/E stocks generally show slightly superior risk-adjusted results.

Comments and Interpretation

Most surprising is the low market risk associated with high P/E stocks and the high market risk associated with low P/E stocks. The Beta statistics for groups 4, 5, and 6—the three groups of twenty-five stocks with the highest P/E ratio—were between 0.72 and 1.00. In contrast, the Beta statistics for groups 1, 2, and 3—the three groups of twenty-five stocks with the lowest P/E ratio—were between 1.0 and 1.49. This high Beta for low P/E stocks is evident in the three of the four years of market declines when group 1—the group of twenty-five stocks with the lowest P/E ratios—failed to outperform the market. Specifically, in 1957 when the market declined 9.9 percent, the low P/E's declined 14.5 percent; in 1966 when the market went down 8.6 percent, the low P/E's declined 9.7 percent; and in 1969 when the market suffered a 14.0 percent loss, the low P/E's dropped 24.8 percent. In only one year in which the market declined—1962—did low P/E stocks outperform the market. Such a record refutes the commonly held notion that low P/E stocks offer superior defensive characteristics in market declines.

On the other hand, low P/E stocks usually outperformed the market in market advances. In every one of the thirteen years of market advances between 1954 and 1970, low P/E stocks showed superior returns.

---

[a]The numerator of the P/E ratio used in this study was the average high/low price of the stock for the year. The denominator used was earnings reported for the prior year. If the earnings were below $0.30 per share, the P/E was not calculated.

Table 4-1
Stocks Ranked by P/E Ratio

One Year–Close to Close

Statistical Data	Lowest 1	2	3	Middle	4	Highest 5	6
Return-Group	23.24	18.70	19.92	17.08	11.46	14.21	15.76
Return-All	17.29	17.29	17.29	17.29	17.29	17.29	17.29
Pct Over	50.12	45.88	46.82	44.09	36.71	37.41	44.24
Beta	1.27	1.13	1.10	.97	.82	.85	.86
Std Err Beta	.06	.07	.05	.02	.05	.13	.13
Std Err Alpha	1.64	2.06	1.44	.60	1.39	3.63	3.68
R Squared	96.89	94.01	96.82	99.26	94.72	74.02	74.09
T Value	21.63	15.34	21.37	44.90	16.41	6.54	6.55
Geom Mean	1.200	1.159	1.174	1.152	1.099	1.122	1.136
Std Dev Group	28.35	25.69	24.62	21.45	18.47	21.72	22.03
Std Err Est	5.32	6.69	4.67	1.96	4.52	11.79	11.94

Composite Measures	1	2	3		4	5	6
Alpha	1.35	-.83	.92	.37	-2.64	-.44	.89
Sharpe Index	.82	.73	.81	.80	.62	.65	.72
Treynor Index	18.36	16.55	18.13	17.67	14.05	16.77	18.33
Down Mkt Index	-1.07	.74	-.84	-.38	3.23	.52	-1.04

Table 4-2
Stocks Ranked by P/E Ratio

Two Years—Close to Close

Statistical Data	Lowest			Middle	Highest		
	1	2	3		4	5	6
Return-Group	44.94	40.15	36.74	31.91	24.75	24.45	32.56
Return-All	33.22	33.22	33.22	33.22	33.22	33.22	33.22
Pct Over	49.41	48.00	47.53	40.41	32.00	35.76	42.12
Beta	1.49	1.27	1.08	.94	.82	.72	.88
Std Err Beta	.10	.10	.05	.02	.08	.11	.14
Std Err Alpha	4.21	4.65	2.19	1.08	3.65	4.68	6.21
R Squared	94.25	90.67	96.91	99.00	86.75	75.47	72.37
T Value	15.68	12.07	21.71	38.46	9.91	6.79	6.27
Geom Mean	1.385	1.350	1.332	1.291	1.221	1.221	1.292
Std Dev Group	44.99	38.94	31.97	27.58	25.68	24.19	30.25
Std Err Est	11.48	12.66	5.98	2.94	9.95	12.75	16.93

Composite Measures	1	2	3		4	5	6
Alpha	-4.63	-1.93	1.02	.76	-2.39	.60	3.35
Sharpe Index	1.00	1.03	1.15	1.16	.96	1.01	1.08
Treynor Index	30.12	31.69	34.17	34.03	30.30	34.05	37.03
Down Mkt Index	3.10	1.52	-.95	-.81	2.92	-.83	-3.81

Table 4-3
Stocks Ranked by P/E Ratio

One Year-Ave. High/Low

Statistical Data	*Lowest*			*Middle*		*Highest*	
	1	2	3	4		5	6
Return-Group	14.80	12.99	14.41	14.54	12.72	15.83	18.04
Return-All	14.67	14.67	14.67	14.67	14.67	14.67	14.67
Pct Over	44.00	41.65	45.88	44.07	41.65	44.00	50.82
Beta	1.14	1.03	1.00	1.01	.85	.79	1.00
Std Err Beta	.09	.08	.06	.03	.07	.15	.11
Std Err Alpha	1.85	1.59	1.30	.63	1.37	3.10	2.17
R Squared	91.27	92.01	94.31	98.64	91.46	64.41	85.45
T Value	12.52	13.14	15.76	32.93	12.68	5.21	9.39
Geom Mean	1.135	1.120	1.134	1.136	1.120	1.150	1.170
Std Dev Group	16.80	15.13	14.58	14.39	12.55	13.94	15.28
Std Err Est	5.29	4.55	3.70	1.79	3.90	8.85	6.20

Composite Measures	1	2	3	4		5	6
Alpha	-1.89	-2.10	-.32	-.31	.24	4.19	3.36
Sharpe Index	.88	.86	.99	1.01	1.01	1.14	1.18
Treynor Index	13.01	12.63	14.35	14.36	14.96	19.96	18.03
Down Mkt Index	1.66	2.04	.32	.31	-.28	-5.29	-3.36

Note the low Beta effects when analyzing high P/E stocks, group 6, Table 4-1. In the four years of market declines, high P/E stocks outperformed the market in three of these years, namely, 1957, 1966, and 1969. In 1962, again the exception, high P/E stocks declined 26.2 percent compared to 13.2 percent for the market. But in the thirteen years of market advances, the market outperformed high P/E stocks seven times compared to none for low P/E stocks. Therefore, as measured by the Beta statistic, a portfolio manager should structure his investments toward low P/E stocks if anticipating a market advance.

The lower market risk of high P/E stocks is somewhat offset by higher unique risk. Although the evidence is not as consistent as that found in the market-risk (Beta) measurements, the standard error of estimate tended to be somewhat higher and the R-squared tended to be somewhat lower for high P/E stocks. This higher unique risk is found, for example, in group 6 (Table 4-1), which showed a standard error of 11.9 and an R-squared of only 74.1 percent. In contrast, low P/E stocks in group 1 (Table 4-1) showed a standard error of 5.3 and an R-squared of 96.9 percent. The least unique risk, as measured by the standard error, was found in the middle P/E groups.

The first implication of this higher unique risk and lower market risk of high P/E stocks is that security analysts should be more concerned with the individual company than with the general market when recommending high P/E stocks for purchase. In contrast, an analyst recommending a low P/E stock should rely more on market expectations.

The second implication of this higher unique risk is that portfolios composed of high P/E stocks are not completely diversified. That is, as a group they respond somewhat independent of the market. This incomplete diversification suggests that for high P/E stocks one should construct a portfolio with more than twenty-five stocks.

The three measures of internal consistency—namely, the standard deviation, the mean absolute deviation, and the percentage of the number of returns which outperformed the market—tend to favor low P/E stocks. Again, the exception to this finding is the case where returns are calculated using the average high/low price of the stock. But combining both instances where returns are calculated using year-end prices over both one- and two-year time horizons, the percentage of the number of low P/E stocks which outperformed the market fluctuated between 45 and 50; in contrast, the corresponding interval for high P/E stocks was between 32 and 44.

Results—The P/E Ratio Coupled with Earnings Increase

The evidence shown in Tables 4-4, 4-5 and 4-6 suggests that if companies reporting an earnings decline are excluded from the sample:

1. *Risk*. Low P/E stocks still exhibit more market risk and less unique risk than high P/E stocks, but the market risk is not as great as that for all low P/E companies.
2. *Return*. If performance is measured over one- and two-year periods using year-end prices, low P/E stocks show higher returns than that for high P/E stocks; but if the average high/low price is used to calculate returns, high P/E stocks show slightly superior returns.
3. *Risk-adjusted Results*. On a risk-adjusted, one-parameter basis, the group of twenty-five stocks with the highest P/E ratio show superior results.

Comments and Interpretation—The P/E Ratio Coupled with Earnings Increase

The results of eliminating companies that had an earnings decline were most dramatic in group 6, the group of stocks with the highest P/E ratio. In each time period the four composite risk-adjusted measures of group 6 showed superior performance. For example, consider one of these measures, the Alpha statistic, for group 6:

| | Alpha (High P/E Stocks) | |
| | All High | Coupled with |
Pricing Period	*P/E Stocks*	*Earnings Increase*
One Year—Close to Close	0.89	4.91
Two Years—Close to Close	3.35	8.93
One Year—Average High/Low	3.36	6.99

Note that in each of the three pricing periods, a higher Alpha was obtained for high P/E stocks after eliminating companies which reported an earnings decline. While the returns of this group were not always superior to those of low P/E groups, the market risk was substantially lower.

The evidence that a superior risk-adjusted return can be obtained in high P/E stocks is perhaps not surprising to many large financial institutions; but the interaction of risk and return of these high P/E stocks is not usually understood. That is, superior risk-adjusted performance of high P/E stocks is due almost entirely to the reduction of market risk rather than to an increase in returns. This finding is not at all consistent with those analysts who argue that high P/E stocks are closely related to high market risk. However, it is consistent with those analysts who argue that stocks with a high P/E have not always generated higher returns.

On a year-by-year analysis, the returns from the stocks in group 6 show

Table 4-4
Stocks Ranked by P/E Ratio, Earnings Increase

One Year–Close to Close

Statistical Data	Lowest			Middle	Highest		
	1	2	3		4	5	6
Return-Group	19.09	14.89	17.86	13.34	13.44	11.49	16.67
Return-All	14.77	14.77	14.77	14.77	14.77	14.77	14.77
Pct Over	47.75	44.00	49.25	40.54	42.75	37.50	47.50
Beta	1.17	1.00	.97	.91	.78	.90	.80
Std Err Beta	.07	.07	.09	.07	.08	.14	.16
Std Err Alpha	1.82	1.77	2.36	1.68	1.90	3.51	4.05
R Squared	94.90	93.48	88.27	92.91	88.34	74.58	63.35
T Value	16.14	14.17	10.26	13.55	10.30	6.41	4.92
Geom Mean	1.167	1.129	1.160	1.118	1.122	1.096	1.149
Std Dev Group	24.31	20.99	20.81	19.01	16.83	21.02	20.23
Std Err Est	5.87	5.73	7.62	5.41	6.14	11.33	13.09

Composite Measures

	1	2	3		4	5	6
Alpha	1.78	.05	3.57	-.05	1.88	-1.78	4.91
Sharpe Index	.79	.71	.86	.70	.80	.55	.82
Treynor Index	16.29	14.82	18.46	14.71	17.17	12.79	20.93
Down Mkt Index	-1.52	-.05	-3.69	.06	-2.40	1.98	-6.16

Table 4-5
Stocks Ranked by P/E Ratio, Earnings Increase

Two Years–Close to Close

Statistical Data	Lowest			Middle	Highest	
	1	*2*	*3*	*4*	*5*	*6*
Return-Group	39.35	32.93	34.87	23.90	23.64	30.67
Return-All	29.47	29.47	29.47	29.47	29.47	29.47
Pct Over	49.50	48.00	48.25	35.28	35.75	45.50
Beta	1.34	1.01	.96	.84	.86	.74
Std Err Beta	.10	.12	.12	.10	.16	.17
Std Err Alpha	3.90	4.55	4.57	4.06	6.26	6.66
R Squared	92.90	84.52	82.84	82.48	67.34	57.43
T Value	13.53	8.74	8.22	8.12	5.37	4.35
Geom Mean	1.351	1.300	1.321	1.217	1.207	1.281
Std Dev Group	36.13	28.57	27.27	23.93	27.07	25.22
Std Err Est	10.29	12.02	12.08	10.71	16.54	17.59

Composite Measures	*1*	*2*	*3*	*4*	*5*	*6*
Alpha	-.26	3.06	6.64	-.83	-1.63	8.93
Sharpe Index	1.09	1.15	1.28	1.00	.87	1.22
Treynor Index	29.28	32.48	36.40	28.48	27.56	41.57
Down Mkt Index	.19	-3.02	-6.93	.98	1.90	-12.11

Table 4-6
Stocks Ranked by P/E Ratio, Earnings Increase

One Year-Ave High/Low

Statistical Data	Lowest		Middle		Highest	
	1	2	3	4	5	6
Return-Group	12.82	12.21	14.24	13.84	14.33	19.60
Return-All	13.61	13.61	13.61	13.61	13.61	13.61
Pct Over	43.25	42.25	45.50	47.00	45.25	56.75
Beta	.98	.84	1.00	.86	.86	.93
Std Err Beta	.10	.09	.11	.07	.15	.17
Std Err Alpha	2.00	1.83	2.05	1.44	2.91	3.21
R Squared	86.74	85.01	86.57	90.63	70.19	69.20
T Value	9.57	8.91	9.50	11.63	5.74	5.61
Geom Mean	1.118	1.115	1.132	1.131	1.134	1.185
Std Dev Croup	14.64	12.60	14.95	12.55	14.23	15.45
Std Err Est	5.70	5.22	5.86	4.11	8.31	9.17
Composite Measures	1	2	3	4	5	6
Alpha	-.55	.81	.59	2.12	2.63	6.99
Sharpe Index	.88	.97	.95	1.10	1.01	1.27
Treynor Index	13.05	14.58	14.20	16.07	16.68	21.16
Down Mkt Index	.56	-.97	-.59	-2.46	-3.07	-7.55

ROCKHURST COLLEGE LIBRARY

superior defensive characteristics. In 1957 when the market declined 9.9 percent, group 6 stocks advanced 0.1 percent; in 1966 when the market fell 8.6 percent, group 6 stocks increased 2.6 percent; and in 1969 when the market declined 14.0 percent this group appreciated a surprising 15.2 percent. Only in 1962, when the market fell 13.2 percent did this group fail to exhibit defensive characteristics.

Conclusion

If composite risk-adjusted measures are ignored, it is evident that low P/E stocks offer higher returns than high P/E stocks—a result for the most part consistent with that of other researchers. But in terms of both risk and return, the results contradict the implications of most of the prior studies mentioned at the beginning of this chapter, that is, that low P/E stocks are "better" investments.

But P/E's may not be enough. Let us now turn to Chapter 5 where the growth rate is examined in terms of investment results.

5

Earnings Growth and Investment Results

While Chapter 4 described the empirical risk/return relation between the P/E ratio and investment results, this chapter examines the relation between earnings growth and investment results. Models of this type are referred to as "price indifferent" for they imply that growth, irrespective of price, is important.

One major problem, in studying the relation between earnings growth and investment results is the choice of the parameters in the growth equation. For example, what historic time period should be used to calculate growth? If a firm increases its earnings in one year, is this growth? And how does one calculate growth if more than one year is involved? Should a compound rate be used? or arithmetic? or least squares? Moreover, should growth be based only on earnings? or should sales, assets, or some other variable be used?

For purposes of this study, two growth calculations are made. In the first case, earnings growth is defined simply as the percentage increase in a company's earnings over the prior year. The twenty-five companies showing the smallest percentage change, usually negative, were assigned to group 1; and the twenty-five companies which reported the largest percentage change were placed in group 6. In both cases, companies reporting less than $0.30 per share in earnings were deleted from the sample to avoid the exaggerated performance when computing percentages from a low base.

In the second growth computation, a four-year compound growth rate is used. This second calculation was added because the shorter one-year period in the first study tended to penalize companies that were longer-term oriented. Group 1 includes companies with the smallest growth rate and group 6 comprises companies with the highest growth rate. The hypothesis, as before, is that these historic growth rates, whether calculated for either a one-year or four-year period, have no inherent value in determining risk-adjusted performance.

Prior Studies on Earnings Growth

Robert Levy and Spero Kripotos

Levy and Kripotos provide evidence that earnings growth is a relevant

49

variable in achieving superior investment results but that the P/E is of minor importance. In their concluding remarks, Levy and Kripotos state:

These studies suggest that price/earnings ratios are of comparatively little use as a primary method of selecting securities, or as a means of further refining a list of stocks initially selected by either relative price strength or earnings growth. In our opinion, however, relative price strength and earnings growth are of major significance for purposes of security selection, and that the combination of both measures is capable of producing results superior to the use of either alone.[1]

The data base used by Levy and Kripotos included month-end prices and quarterly earnings for 295 companies over the period 1957-64. Companies with fiscal years ending in March, June, September, and December, and companies reporting a loss over any four consecutive quarters were excluded. Earnings growth was defined as the percentage change of the latest twelve-month earnings; and earnings were assumed to be reported one month after the close of the quarter. The P/E was computed as the current month-end price divided by the latest twelve-month earnings.

The most significant results of this study were that the twenty-six-week returns of the stock of companies showing the largest percentage increase in earnings averaged 10.0 percent compared to only 3.2 percent for the stock of companies reporting the smallest increase. If the stock of companies reporting the highest growth is further subdivided by the value of their P/E ratio, it is seen that the results are mixed, thereby implying that high-growth stocks give superior results irrespective of what an investor must pay in terms of a P/E ratio.

With regard to the absolute value of the P/E ratio, Levy and Kripotos find some evidence that low P/E stocks produce higher returns than high P/E stocks, a result consistent with the evidence presented in Chapter 4, but also find that this ratio is not as important as earnings growth or relative strength.

O. Maurice Joy and Charles P. Jones

Joy and Jones present evidence to support the hypothesis that the P/E ratio and earnings growth, both figures being known to the financial community, have predictive value.[2] The data used by Joy and Jones included the quarterly stock prices and earnings of 300 companies for the period 1962-66. Excluded from this data base were companies whose fiscal quarters ended in months other than March, June, September, and December; also excluded were companies reporting a deficit.

While the main subject of the Joy and Jones study was to question the conclusions of the aforementioned Levy-Kripotos study, that is, minimizing the importance of the P/E ratio in comparison to earnings growth and relative strength, Joy and Jones show that both the P/E *and* earnings growth are important. By redefining the denominator to include only the prior quarter's earnings rather than the prior twelve-month earnings, Joy and Jones present the following evidence supporting the use of the P/E ratio in an investment decision.

Variable	Group	Return	Std Dev
High P/E	1	4.4%	14.6
	2	4.9	13.0
	3	6.2	15.2
	4	7.5	12.4
Low P/E	5	12.1	15.9
High Growth	1	12.6	17.8
	2	8.5	12.6
	3	5.9	11.0
	4	5.1	11.8
Low Growth	5	3.0	16.3

The results of the Joy-Jones study show that low P/E ratios as well as high earnings growth are indicators of superior investment returns.

Victor Niederhoffer and Patrick J. Regan

Niederhoffer and Regan present evidence on the value of analysts' earnings forecasts, that is, growth expectations, but do not link their findings to a P/E ratio.[3] The authors examined the earnings changes of the top and bottom fifty performers during 1970. The earnings forecasts used were found in the March 31, 1970, publication of the Standard & Poor's "Earnings Forecaster," generally recognized as a consensus forecast by leading institutions; and these estimates were compared to the actual 1970 earnings figures reported in 1971. By comparing the accuracy of the forecast to actual 1970 performance of the stock price, the authors could evaluate the worth of accurate earnings forecasts.

Their conclusions reflect the principle that accurate forecasts are useful in achieving superior investment results. They conclude:

In sum, the results of this study demonstrate that stock prices are strongly dependent on earnings changes, both absolute and relative to analysts' estimates. The common characteristics of the companies registering the best price changes included a forecast of moderately increased earnings and a realized profit gain in excess of analysts' expectations. The worst-performing stocks were characterized by severe earnings declines, combined with unusually optimistic forecasts.[4]

The results of this study are useful to an analyst in selecting stocks for further analysis. But contrary to the usual procedure of selecting stocks of companies which are generally thought to show the largest increase in earnings, according to their study, the analyst should concentrate on those issues which show only a modest increase in estimated earnings. If the analyst finds that the consensus earnings are low, then the analyst should recommend the stock.

Note that this selection procedure is a compromise between the use of data generally known to the financial community, that is, the consensus forecasts, and data not yet known, that is, actual earnings figures. As such, this study helps to identify a balance between the use of historic information as contrasted to information not yet known. But if earnings and growth rates cannot be forecast, as suggested by some studies,[5] then one must rely on known data.

Charles P. Jones

Jones studied the relation between earnings trends and investment performance using quarterly data.[6] His hypothesis was that reported quarterly earnings which are significantly better than those anticipated by market professionals tend to generate intermediate stock price trends. To prove the hypothesis, he assumed that earnings anticipated by market professionals approximated a straight line projected from the prior eight quarters of reported earnings. If the actual reported earnings exceeded this projection by at least 1.5 standard errors, the stock was "bought" two months after the end of the quarter. The performance of these stocks was then followed over the next six months. The time period covered was from 1965 to June 1969, and the number of stocks in the sample was 416.

In addition to the standard-error criterion, the stocks having a P/E ratio greater than that of the S & P 425 were excluded. This additional refinement was necessary, according to the author, because the price adjustment for these stocks had already taken place.

The results of Jones' test after adjusting for risk, that is, using both the Treynor and the Sharpe Index, suggest that "quarterly earnings reports have information content affecting the fundamental worth of a common stock." The stocks selected using Jones' criteria resulted in relatively high values in both the Treynor and the Sharpe Index. Even better risk-adjusted returns were shown by ranking the stocks by their P/E ratio; however, the author advises that the disadvantage of this strategy is that information on a large number of stocks is required. If earnings alone are used, then decisions can be made at the time that earnings are reported. In any case, Jones finds that growth, irrespective of price, is important.

Results—One-Year Earnings Growth[a]

The empirical evidence presented in Tables 5-1, 5-2, and 5-3 on earnings growth and investment results suggests that:

1. *Risk*. The stock-price returns of both the extreme high-growth and the extreme low- or negative-growth companies exhibit high market risk. Furthermore, high-growth companies contain relatively high unique risk.
2. *Return*. The extreme high-growth companies, group 6, show higher returns than the other groups.
3. *Risk-adjusted Results*. On a risk-adjusted, one-parameter basis, the results tend to favor the middle to high-growth groups; somewhat inferior risk-adjusted performance was found in the low-growth groups.

Comment and Interpretation

The high market risk found in the common stocks of the high-growth (group 6) and the low-growth (group 1) companies is not particularly surprising for these companies most likely show the highest earnings variability. The Beta statistics for the common stocks of low-growth companies fluctuated between 1.13 and 1.21, depending on the time horizon; and the Beta range for that of the high-growth companies was between 1.13 and 1.27. In contrast, the Betas for the middle groups were between 0.86 and 0.95.

In the four years of market downturns (1957, 1962, 1966, 1969), both groups of stocks of companies showing the largest as well as the smallest increase in earnings performed worse than the market. The group with the smallest increase in earnings (group 1) performed worse than the market in three of these four years, and the group with the largest increase in earnings (group 6) performed worse in all four years.

But the performance of these two groups is somewhat different during the twelve years of market advances. While the group of stocks of companies reporting the smallest increase in earnings outperformed the market only five times, the group of stocks of companies reporting the largest increase outperformed the market ten times. But note that this superior return of high-growth stocks in advancing markets is also accompanied by more unique risk. For example, as shown in Table 5-1, the standard error of

[a]Earnings growth is calculated as the percentage change in reported earnings from year t - 1 to year t. Group 1 contains the companies which had little or no growth; group 6 contains those which reported superior growth. Note that only earnings' growth is being considered; the P/E ratio relative to earnings' growth is examined in Chapter 6.

Table 5-1
Stocks Ranked by One-Year Earnings Growth

One Year–Close to Close

Statistical Data	1	Lowest 2	3	Middle	4	Highest 5	6
Return-Group	13.95	15.00	13.18	13.88	15.96	13.68	18.35
Return-All	14.77	14.77	14.77	14.77	14.77	14.77	14.77
Pct Over	41.25	44.75	43.50	43.60	46.50	41.75	43.00
Beta	1.13	1.09	.86	.89	.96	.99	1.27
Std Err Beta	.08	.10	.10	.02	.12	.11	.11
Std Err Alpha	2.11	2.49	2.43	.59	2.94	2.64	2.87
R Squared	92.79	89.62	84.89	99.03	82.69	86.32	89.74
T Value	13.42	11.00	8.87	37.84	8.18	9.40	11.06
Geom Mean	1.115	1.127	1.115	1.124	1.141	1.115	1.151
Std Dev Group	23.71	23.32	18.92	18.03	21.31	21.54	27.11
Std Err Est	6.81	8.03	7.86	1.90	9.48	8.52	9.28

Composite Measures	1	2	3		4	5	6
Alpha	-2.74	-1.14	.44	.77	1.79	-.95	-.41
Sharpe Index	.59	.64	.70	.77	.75	.63	.68
Treynor Index	12.34	13.73	15.28	15.64	16.64	13.81	14.44
Down Mkt Index	2.43	1.04	-.51	-.87	-1.87	.96	.33

Table 5-2

Stocks Ranked by One-Year Earnings Growth

Two Years–Close to Close

Statistical Data	Lowest 1	2	3	Middle 4	Highest 5	6
Return-Group	31.16	29.54	26.50	27.16	27.85	32.46
Return-All	29.47	29.47	29.47	29.47	29.47	29.47
Pct Over	40.25	40.00	38.75	41.66	38.50	41.50
Beta	1.21	1.20	.92	.86	.83	1.13
Std Err Beta	.13	.14	.10	.04	.15	.15
Std Err Alpha	4.98	5.57	3.73	1.57	5.84	5.69
R Squared	86.71	83.57	86.93	97.03	68.74	81.16
T Value	9.56	8.44	9.65	21.40	5.55	7.77
Geom Mean	1.269	1.256	1.241	1.252	1.253	1.283
Std Dev Group	33.78	33.95	25.49	22.59	25.81	32.40
Std Err Est	13.16	14.71	9.85	4.16	15.43	15.04

Composite Measures	1	2	3	4	5	6
Alpha	-4.62	-5.77	-.53	1.82	3.51	-.74
Sharpe Index	.92	.87	1.04	1.07	1.08	1.00
Treynor Index	25.67	24.65	28.89	31.22	33.72	28.81
Down Mkt Index	3.80	4.82	.58	-1.75	-4.26	.66

Table 5-3
Stocks Ranked by One-Year Earnings Growth

One Year–Ave High/Low

Statistical Data	*Lowest*			*Middle*		*Highest*	
	1	2	3		4	5	6
Return-Group	13.28	11.17	12.68	13.03	13.96	13.61	18.28
Return-All	13.61	13.61	13.61	13.61	13.61	13.61	13.61
Pct Over	43.25	38.25	41.00	44.94	42.75	44.75	49.25
Beta	1.19	1.02	1.07	.95	.82	.98	1.17
Std Err Beta	.10	.09	.10	.02	.10	.11	.13
Std Err Alpha	2.03	1.80	1.91	.46	2.02	2.17	2.53
R Squared	90.28	89.57	89.35	99.12	81.64	84.74	85.26
T Value	11.40	10.97	10.84	39.82	7.89	8.82	9.00
Geom Mean	1.119	1.101	1.116	1.122	1.132	1.126	1.169
Std Dev Group	17.38	14.91	15.66	13.23	12.58	14.83	17.60
Std Err Est	5.79	5.15	5.46	1.32	5.76	6.20	7.22

Composite Measures	1	2	3		4	5	6
Alpha	-2.92	-2.68	-1.84	.11	2.80	.21	2.34
Sharpe Index	.76	.75	.81	.99	1.11	.92	1.04
Treynor Index	11.16	10.98	11.89	13.73	17.04	13.83	15.61
Down Mkt Index	2.46	2.63	1.72	-.12	-3.42	-.21	-2.00

estimate of annual returns for the group of stocks of companies showing the smallest increase in earnings was 6.81 while that of companies showing the largest increase in earnings was 9.28.

The results as measured by the one-parameter indicators—that is, Alpha, Sharpe Index, Treynor Index, and the Down Market Index suggest that superior risk-adjusted performance is found in the middle to high-growth groups. Note that in groups 1, 2, and 3, the three twenty-five-stock portfolios of companies reporting the smallest increase in earnings, the Alpha is negative in eight of nine times over the three different time horizons. But in groups 4, 5, and 6, the three twenty-five-stock portfolios of companies reporting the largest increase in earnings, the Alpha is positive six out of nine times. In addition, the middle group shows a positive Alpha in all of the three time periods.

With regard to internal consistency, as measured by the standard deviation of the group, the mean absolute deviation and the percentage of the number of stocks which outperform the market, the results tend to favor the middle group; and the stocks of companies showing the largest earnings gain tend to show a slight superiority over those of companies showing the smallest earnings gain. Furthermore, as measured by the standard deviation and the mean absolute deviation, the middle group showed consistently lower variability within the groups.

Results—Four-Year Earnings Growth

The empirical evidence presented in Tables 5-4, 5-5, and 5-6 suggests the following:

1. *Risk*. As in the one-year earnings growth study, an investment in both the extreme high-growth and the extreme low- or negative-growth companies incurs high market risk. However, unlike the results of the one-year earnings growth study, an investment in the high-growth companies does not exhibit a high unique risk.
2. *Return*. Similar to the one-year earnings study, higher returns are found in the high-growth companies.
3. *Risk-adjusted Results*. On a risk-adjusted basis, the results favor the middle groups.

Comment and Interpretation—Four-Year Earnings Growth

The most significant similarity between the one-year and the four-year

Table 5-4
Stocks Ranked by Four-Year Earnings Growth, Lagged One Year

One Year—Close to Close

Statistical Data	Lowest			Middle	Highest		
	1	2	3		4	5	6
Return-Group	14.14	11.43	12.76	13.33	15.91	16.10	16.97
Return-All	14.49	14.49	14.49	14.49	14.49	14.49	14.49
Pct Over	43.71	40.86	41.14	43.37	48.00	44.57	42.86
Beta	1.17	.99	.89	.87	.90	1.20	1.23
Std Err Beta	.11	.07	.08	.02	.08	.10	.09
Std Err Alpha	2.94	1.81	2.03	.58	2.11	2.70	2.42
R Squared	89.83	94.33	91.49	99.20	91.01	91.69	93.53
T Value	10.30	14.13	11.36	38.51	11.02	11.50	13.17
Geom Mean	1.110	1.093	1.110	1.118	1.141	1.129	1.137
Std Dev Group	26.44	21.84	19.96	18.72	20.21	26.87	27.30
Std Err Est	9.11	5.62	6.29	1.81	6.55	8.37	7.50

Composite Measures	1	2	3		4	5	6
Alpha	-2.78	-2.89	-.13	.75	2.90	-1.26	-.85
Sharpe Index	.53	.52	.64	.71	.79	.60	.62
Treynor Index	12.11	11.57	14.34	15.35	17.71	13.43	13.80
Down Mkt Index	2.38	2.92	.14	-.86	-3.22	1.05	.69

Table 5-5
Stocks Ranked by Four-Year Earnings Growth, Lagged One Year

Two Years—Close to Close

Statistical Data	Lowest			Middle	Highest		
	1	2	3		4	5	6
Return-Group	34.34	28.44	28.40	28.32	32.92	33.12	38.42
Return-All	31.21	31.21	31.21	31.21	31.21	31.21	31.21
Pct Over	40.29	40.57	40.86	39.90	43.71	43.43	43.43
Beta	1.10	1.03	.89	.85	1.06	1.07	1.27
Std Err Beta	.20	.09	.10	.03	.13	.11	.14
Std Err Alpha	7.99	3.67	4.26	1.39	5.43	4.58	5.70
R Squared	72.39	91.63	85.77	98.14	84.07	88.41	87.40
T Value	5.61	11.47	8.50	25.13	7.96	9.57	9.12
Geom Mean	1.301	1.255	1.260	1.264	1.296	1.297	1.334
Std Dev Group	34.03	28.36	25.24	22.69	30.44	30.11	35.87
Std Err Est	19.31	8.86	10.29	3.35	13.13	11.07	13.76

Composite Measures	1	2	3		4	5	6
Alpha	.09	-3.68	.74	1.73	-.11	-.38	-1.25
Sharpe Index	1.01	1.00	1.13	1.25	1.08	1.10	1.07
Treynor Index	31.29	27.63	32.04	33.23	31.11	30.85	30.22
Down Mkt Index	-.08	3.58	-.84	-2.02	.10	.35	.99

Table 5-6

Stocks Ranked by Four-Year Earnings Growth, Lagged One Year

One Year–Ave High/Low

Statistical Data	*Lowest*			*Middle*	*Highest*		
	1	2	3		4	5	6
Return-Group	11.68	7.89	9.65	11.36	13.66	12.85	12.08
Return-All	11.76	11.76	11.76	11.76	11.76	11.76	11.76
Pct Over	42.86	36.00	39.14	44.29	48.29	45.71	45.14
Beta	1.17	.99	1.07	.89	1.02	1.02	1.20
Std Err Beta	.14	.09	.09	.03	.10	.13	.15
Std Err Alpha	2.56	1.59	1.52	.51	1.74	2.29	2.74
R Squared	84.85	91.22	92.89	98.76	90.06	83.93	83.69
T Value	8.20	11.16	12.52	30.96	10.43	7.92	7.85
Geom Mean	1.103	1.069	1.086	1.107	1.127	1.118	1.106
Std Dev Group	17.14	13.95	14.90	12.01	14.40	14.93	17.71
Std Err Est	7.20	4.47	4.29	1.44	4.90	6.46	7.73

Composite Measures	1	2	3		4	5	6
Alpha	-2.13	-3.76	-2.91	.93	1.71	.89	-2.08
Sharpe Index	.68	.57	.65	.95	.95	.86	.68
Treynor Index	9.95	7.96	9.04	12.81	13.45	12.64	10.03
Down Mkt Index	1.81	3.80	2.73	-1.04	-1.69	-.88	1.73

results is the superior risk-adjusted performance of the middle group. While this slightly better performance could have been due to chance, it is interesting that the trend toward the middle minimizes the longer-term importance of highly favorable one-year earnings reports. But note that as the middle group increases in importance, the highest year-to-year returns—unadjusted for risk—are still found in the highest-growth group (Tables 5-1 and 5-4). Over a two-year holding period, this superiority is not as evident. Therefore short-term traders willing to take risk should concentrate on those companies reporting the highest growth rates. On the other hand, investors seeking superior risk-adjusted performance on a longer-term basis should concentrate on those companies showing a moderate growth rate.

Conclusion

While prior studies mentioned in the beginning of this chapter suggest that earnings growth, irrespective of price, may be a dominant determinant of stock-price returns, the results of this study suggest that on a risk-adjusted basis the middle group contains the superior investments. If risk is ignored, this study does support the findings of these prior studies since superior returns are in fact found in stocks of those companies that have reported the highest growth rates in earnings. On balance, however, it is not at all clear that the higher expected returns are worth the additional risks involved.

In this respect, one major implication of these results is that the "turn-around situation," usually a company which has reported inferior results for the prior year, should be avoided. That is, the turnaround search is likely to result not only in inferior returns relative to the market but also in substantially more risk.

In looking at this summary data, one might be tempted to argue that these results are inconsistent with those presented in Chapter 4. In that chapter, it was found that high returns were not found in the high P/E groups. This apparent inconsistency is resolved when one realizes that the companies reporting the largest increase in annual earnings are also likely to have the lowest P/E ratio. Accordingly both low P/E stocks *and* the highest growth companies, as measured by their one-year percentage increase in earnings, show both higher returns and higher risks.

The problem here however is that earnings growth by itself is considered in relation to investment results. As such, the investment decision is "price indifferent," a concept largely rejected by most financial theorists and practicing analysts. Let us now introduce a relationship between growth and the P/E ratio—one suggested by Graham et al., although somewhat modified—and analyze the investment results.

6

Graham's Valuation Formula and Investment Results

The controversy over whether the P/E ratio or growth is the dominant factor in generating superior returns has been examined in various studies mentioned in Chapters 4 and 5. The evidence presented there suggests that (1) high P/E's if coupled with an increase in earnings and (2) average growth rates are two ratios indicative of superior risk-adjusted performance.

This chapter is concerned with the investment results of a combination of the growth rate and the P/E ratio—and the one used is a modification of that suggested by Graham, Dodd, and Cottle.[1] In this sense, it is seen that the real issue confronting the P/E ratio versus growth-rate controversy now shifts from an analysis of each one individually to a combination of the two; that is, how much should one pay for growth?

Graham et al. present their views on a justifiable P/E ratio, depending on the company's growth rate, but readily admit that their mathematical techniques contain an element of "ingrained distrust." Their views, however, can be summed in their table (Table 6-1) expressing P/E as a function of growth rate:

Table 6-1
Graham's Growth Table

Expected rate of growth (for 7 years)	Multiplier of average (fourth-year) earnings	Multiplier of current earnings
3.5%	13x	15x
6.0	14x	17x
7.2	15x	20x
10.0	16x	23.5x
12.0	17x	27x
14.3	18x	31x
17.0	19x	35.5x
20.0	20x	41.5x

Source: Benjamin Graham, David L. Dodd, Sidney Cottle, and Charles Tatham, *Security Analysis, Principles and Technique* (New York: McGraw-Hill Book Co., 1962), p. 537. Used with permission of McGraw-Hill Book Company.

Their second approach, which is tested empirically in this study, describes the growth rate versus P/E relationship as:

$$Value = (8.5 + 2 \times G) \times E$$

where G is the average annual growth rate and E is the current "normal" earnings. (The factor of earnings stability is treated by them as an independent variable which they feel may influence the P/E entirely on its own.)

While guidelines are presented by these authors, they are reluctant to predict results in terms of risk and return. The impression left is that one should purchase stocks which are "undervalued" by their mathematical criterion and sell those which are "overvalued." But, as previously mentioned, Graham et al. do not suggest that these guidelines be used mechanically as done in this study. Certainly, if the guidelines are found to have produced (historically) inferior results, one would hesitate to use them. On the other hand, if found superior when subjected to historical data, perhaps they should be used more frequently by analysts.

Graham does caution his readers on the merits of growth stocks. He states:

When growth-stock experience is viewed as a whole and not simply in the blinding light of IBM's achievements, quite a different picture emerges. One would have expected the general performance of growth stocks in the past two decades to have been decidedly superior to that of the market as a whole, if only because they have steadily increased in market popularity, and thus have had an extra factor to aid their market prices. Available data would indicate that the facts are different from this plausible expectation.[2]

On the other hand, *John R. Andrews* supports the growth-strategy approach and presents some evidence to substantiate his position. His main conclusion is that:

The thesis of this discussion is that the place to be when the market has bottomed is in growth stocks. . . . Over the longer term, properly selected growth investments have been the most rewarding throughout the history of our economy. There is no evidence to support a conclusion that the future will be any different from the past.[3]

In analyzing the performance of growth stocks, Andrews selects his growth stocks with the advantage of hindsight. He finds, for example, that over the past twenty years his sample of quality high-growth issues appreciated 1,222 percent; his quality medium-growth stocks rose 488 percent; and his large industrial group increased 132 percent. Even in 1969, when the Dow Jones Average declined 15.2 percent, his growth stock list appreciated 20 percent. With this and other statistics, he argues that sophisticated investors should develop a strategy of investing in quality, recognized, high-growth stocks.

His performance data are not particularly surprising. While Andrews readily admits that it is most difficult to identify these quality, recognized, high-growth stocks, he does not present data which show that the companies *now* identified as growth issues were, in fact, recognized as growth issues at the beginning of his study. It is a self-fulfilling prophecy to first define a growth stock as one which has had superior earnings growth and then historically prove that the stock of these companies has increased in price. Accordingly, while the evidence does show the superior performance of growth issues during the period 1955-68, the evidence is not particularly convincing because of the use of hindsight in selecting these growth stocks.

Results—Growth of Earnings and the P/E Ratio[a]

The results of this test, Tables 6-2, 6-3 and 6-4 suggest the following:

1. *Risk*. Stocks classified as most undervalued and most overvalued, that is, as reflected in the difference between their theoretical and actual P/E ratio, show both higher market and unique risk.
2. *Return*. Undervalued stocks had significantly higher returns.
3. *Risk-adjusted Results*. On a risk-adjusted basis, undervalued stocks (groups 1, 2, and 3) outperformed those identified as overvalued (groups 4, 5, and 6).

Comment and Interpretation

The evidence supporting the superiority of Graham, Dodd, and Cottle's guidelines is impressive. On a risk-adjusted basis, as measured by any one of the four composite measures (Alpha, Sharpe, Treynor, or the Down Market Index), groups 1, 2, and 3 containing "undervalued" securities outperformed groups 4, 5, and 6 containing "overvalued" securities on an extraordinarily consistent basis. The nine Alphas of each of the groups in each of the three pricing periods were all positive; in contrast, eight of the nine Alphas of the overvalued groups were negative. The remaining

---

[a]A theoretical P/E ratio was first computed from the expression $P/E = 8.5 + 2.0 \times Growth$, where growth is calculated as the four-year compounded return of earnings. This theoretical P/E was then compared to the actual P/E and stocks were ranked on the difference. Group 1 contained the most undervalued stocks according to this criterion and group 6 the most overvalued. Accordingly, the terms *undervalued* and *overvalued* are used to describe these stocks throughout this chapter.

Table 6-2
Stocks Ranked by Graham's Valuation Formula

One Year—Close to Close

Statistical Data	Lowest			Middle	Highest		
	1	2	3		4	5	6
Return-Group	19.48	17.61	16.34	13.52	9.95	10.84	12.74
Return-All	14.49	14.49	14.49	14.49	14.49	14.49	14.49
Pct Over	46.57	45.71	50.57	43.25	40.00	38.86	41.14
Beta	1.21	1.19	.94	.89	.82	.95	1.11
Std Err Beta	.08	.10	.08	.03	.05	.07	.11
Std Err Alpha	2.16	2.70	1.96	.71	1.23	1.69	2.86
R Squared	94.57	91.59	92.80	98.89	96.12	94.67	89.41
T Value	14.46	11.43	12.44	32.76	17.23	14.60	10.06
Geom Mean	1.165	1.144	1.144	1.119	1.085	1.088	1.099
Std Dev Group	26.62	26.77	21.00	19.31	17.95	21.01	25.25
Std Err Est	6.70	8.38	6.09	2.19	3.82	5.24	8.88

Composite Measures	1	2	3		4	5	6
Alpha	2.01	.32	2.68	.56	-1.92	-2.96	-3.38
Sharpe Index	.73	.66	.78	.70	.55	.52	.50
Treynor Index	16.15	14.75	17.33	15.11	12.14	11.38	11.45
Down Mkt Index	-1.66	-.26	-2.84	-.63	2.35	3.11	3.04

Table 6-3
Stocks Ranked by Graham's Valuation Formula

Two Years—Close to Close

Statistical Data	1	Lowest 2	3	Middle 4		Highest 5	6
Return-Group	41.28	37.68	34.55	29.03	23.38	25.42	30.75
Return-All	31.21	31.21	31.21	31.21	31.21	31.21	31.21
Pct Over	45.43	47.43	47.71	39.90	37.14	38.00	37.14
Beta	1.22	1.12	1.03	.91	.71	.96	1.06
Std Err Beta	.12	.13	.10	.04	.07	.08	.18
Std Err Alpha	4.92	5.29	4.28	1.79	2.80	3.27	7.52
R Squared	89.55	86.17	89.00	97.30	89.96	92.29	73.54
T Value	10.14	8.65	9.86	20.80	10.37	11.98	5.78
Geom Mean	1.368	1.341	1.314	1.269	1.218	1.227	1.268
Std Dev Group	34.02	31.80	28.83	24.31	19.79	26.31	32.71
Std Err Est	11.88	12.77	10.33	4.31	6.77	7.89	18.17

Composite Measures	1	2	3	4		5	6
Alpha	3.19	2.75	2.36	.66	1.17	-4.48	-2.44
Sharpe Index	1.21	1.18	1.20	1.19	1.18	.97	.94
Treynor Index	33.82	33.67	33.50	31.93	32.85	26.53	28.92
Down Mkt Index	-2.61	-2.46	-2.29	-.72	-1.64	4.68	2.29

Table 6-4
Stocks Ranked by Graham's Valuation Formula

One Year-Ave High/Low

Statistical Data	Lowest			Middle	Highest		
	1	2	3		4	5	6
Return-Group	14.09	13.81	14.29	11.37	7.14	8.16	10.45
Return-All	11.76	11.76	11.76	11.76	11.76	11.76	11.76
Pct Over	46.57	48.57	50.57	43.95	35.43	38.86	39.14
Beta	1.13	1.09	1.07	.92	.89	1.04	1.10
Std Err Beta	.15	.14	.08	.03	.06	.07	.13
Std Err Alpha	2.64	2.55	1.44	.53	1.11	1.22	2.37
R Squared	82.92	83.02	93.63	98.77	94.44	95.08	85.20
T Value	7.63	7.66	13.28	31.05	14.28	15.23	8.31
Geom Mean	1.128	1.126	1.133	1.106	1.064	1.072	1.092
Std Dev Group	16.69	16.17	14.85	12.39	12.30	14.36	16.05
Std Err Est	7.45	7.20	4.05	1.48	3.13	3.44	6.67

Composite Measures	1	2	3		4	5	6
Alpha	.81	.93	1.72	.60	-3.32	-4.09	-2.50
Sharpe Index	.84	.85	.96	.92	.58	.57	.65
Treynor Index	12.48	12.62	13.38	12.42	8.03	7.84	9.49
Down Mkt Index	-.71	-.85	-1.61	-.65	3.73	3.93	2.27

Sharpe, Treynor, and Down Market Index were all higher in the under-valued situations compared to those in the overvalued groups.

This superior risk-adjusted performance came as a result of higher returns rather than lesser market risk. This finding is important as an alternative to those investors who may want to avoid the "price indifferent" strategy. In this latter strategy, a high risk-adjusted performance was obtained through the combination of lower returns and lower market risks.

On a year-by-year analysis, the evidence again supports the superiority of "undervalued" stocks. It is particularly interesting to compare the performance of these "undervalued" stocks with that of the growth stocks in Chapter 5, particularly in market downturns. In 1957, Chapter 5 growth stocks fell 12.3 percent, undervalued stocks fell 9.2 percent; in 1962, Chapter 5 growth stocks declined 25.0 percent while undervalued stocks were off only 14.8 percent; in the downturns of 1966 and 1969, their performance was about the same. In the ten years when the market did not decline, the "undervalued" stocks equaled or outperformed the growth stocks in nine of these ten years.

Conclusion

The evidence presented in this chapter indicates that superior risk-adjusted returns can be obtained by following the guideline proposed by Graham et al. This guideline suggests that an investor should pay about 8.5 times earnings for the stock of a no-growth company and about 2.0 times earnings for each 1 percent of growth thereafter. Using this mechanical guideline, one can sift through a large number of possible investments and screen those considered most attractive.

So far, the analysis has considered the P/E ratio, growth rates, and one particular combination of growth rate and P/E ratio. Let us now look at some other financial ratios which are typically used by security analysts.

7

Divident Yield and Investment Results

With the exception of the price-earnings ratio and the growth rate, perhaps no other variable has received greater attention by the academic and financial communities than dividends. And it is far from clear what the consensus is regarding the role of dividends. Keep in mind that if one value appears to generate superior risk-adjusted returns, then the market would be deemed inefficient. In this case every investor would buy the stock of the company yielding that particular value, thereby increasing the price of these equities and returning the marketplace to its original random character. If the marketplace is found inefficient in this aspect, the position of Miller and Modigliani (see next section) that dividend policy is irrelevant to the investment decision would not be consistent with this historical evidence.

This chapter considers the risk/return relation between dividend yields and total returns, including capital gains from common stocks. First, the controversy is discussed; second, some differing views are considered; and, third, the results of this study are presented.

The Controversy

In the controversy over the primacy of dividends, there are two schools of thought. One school argues that dividends constitute the main determinant of stock prices, and the other that dividends are not important. The first writer arguing for the primacy of dividends was J.B. Williams in 1938.[1] Williams contended that the value of a particular equity is simply the discounted value of the income stream of the expected dividends. He argued that whether one uses earnings or dividends was not particularly important since earnings and dividends should give the same answer. He states:

If earnings not paid out in dividends are all successfully reinvested at compound interest for the benefit of the stockholder, as the critics imply, then these earnings should produce dividends later; if not, then they are money lost.

The role of dividends took on greater controversy in 1954 when Clendenin and Van Cleave showed that if dividends are discounted at a uniform rate over infinity, and if the growth rate of the dividends exceeds the discount rate, the present value of a stock would be infinity.[2] The authors maintained that while growth rates may in some cases exceed the discount rate, "We have not yet seen any growth stocks marketed at a price of infinity dollars per share." An attempt to resolve this "Petersburg Paradox" was provided by Durand in 1957,[3] but the controversy on how to evaluate growth stocks lingers on.

In 1961 Miller and Modigliani published their classic hypothesis that in valuing equities it is irrelevant whether or not a firm distributes its earnings in the form of dividends.[4] The only factors which may affect this hypothesis, they argue, are items such as an imperfect market, transaction costs, tax differentials, and the predictability of the income stream. Their argument that "dividends don't count" is based on their mathematical proof that any increase in the dividend paid by a company is exactly offset by a decline in the price of the stock.

More recent arguments for the primacy of dividends are provided by authors other than the historical one presented by J.B. Williams. For example, M. Gordon argues that investors prefer the safety of dividend income rather than the risk of capital gains.[5] Because of this preference, Gordon argues, investors tend to discount near-term dividends at a higher rate than they do distant dividends. In such a case, it would appear that, all other factors being equal, near-term dividends are preferable to no dividends.

Some Differing Views

Graham et al.

Graham et al. feel that the role of dividends depends on the type of security being evaluated. They state:

First, in valuing growth shares the dividends can be for all practical purposes ignored and sole reliance placed on expected earnings.

Second, in valuing below-average shares, dividends are of paramount importance. . . .

Third, in valuing shares in the middle group, the role of dividends is still dominant, but the weighting will be less than in the case of the below average shares.[6]

In the second case where dividends are of paramount importance, the guidelines given by Graham et al. in evaluating these shares is as follows:

$$V = M(D + 1/3\ E)$$

where: $V =$ value of the shares.

$M =$ earnings multiples.

$D =$ expected dividends.

$E =$ expected earnings.

From this analysis, Graham et al. state that their own studies

have led to the somewhat surprising conclusion that for typical groups of stocks the weight in market price of $1 of distributed earnings tended to be about four times as great as that of $1 of retained earnings.[7]

While Graham et al. provide these guidelines, they are reluctant to hypothesize that the value of these dividends arbitrarily suggests superior performance either in terms of higher returns or lower risk.

Frederick Amling

Amling hypothesizes that "income common stock" is moderate to low risk and should provide a 7 to 8 percent reward per year.[8] He cautions though that at any given moment of time, the risk/reward relationship may vary.

One major difference between Amling's risk measurement and that used in this study is his standard error of estimate, that is, this author's "unique risk" in contrast to the Beta statistic to measure market risk. Although high Betas are sometimes accompanied by high standard errors, this relationship does not always hold true. In any event, the results of this study do not entirely support Amling's contention that high-income stocks have moderate to low market risk.

Douglas A. Hayes

Hayes lists the prevailing dividend rate as one of his four "quantitative value elements" along with the current level and consistency of earnings, the average level of earnings, and the projected earnings and dividends. His argument for using current dividends and earnings is as follows:

The advantage of current dividends and earnings as value elements is that they represent the most recent tangible evidence of achievement derived from the past managerial policies of the company. In a very real sense, therefore, they constitute the established base from which future dynamic developments must take place. As a result, a tentative indication of the comparative attractiveness of common stocks can often be obtained from a comparison of their prices as ratios of current earnings and dividends.[9]

The implication in Hayes' writings is that high dividend yield is preferable to low dividend yield, other factors being equal. But Hayes does add that this preference must be considered relative to expected growth. Unlike Amling, however, Hayes does not discuss specific risk/reward relationships when commenting on the desirability of these high-yielding stocks.

J. Peter Williamson

Williamson argues that, except in certain legal circumstances where income must be treated separately from capital gains, dividend yield is not a major consideration in the investment decision:

There are still some investors, including some professionals, who think of a portfolio as being either income-oriented or growth-oriented and who focus their attention exclusively on either the dividend yield or the growth rate. But, after all, a dollar is a dollar; what difference does it make whether that dollar is a dividend receipt or a capital appreciation.[10]

Williamson even maintains that the tax advantage of capital gains over dividend income is not particularly relevant for an "after tax dollar is an after tax dollar." So Williamson concludes that segregating dividend yield and capital gains is probably not useful for most investors.

Results—Dividend Yield

The results of this study, presented in Tables 7-1, 7-2, and 7-3 indicate the following:

1. *Risk*. High market and unique risk appear in the lowest dividend playing group (group 1). The groups with the highest dividend yield appear to generate average or slightly above average market risk. And the middle group of stocks—those companies paying about average yield—have the least market risk.
2. *Return*. Significantly higher total returns are found in stocks of companies paying little or no dividends, that is, group 1.
3. *Risk-adjusted Results*. On a risk-adjusted basis, the middle and above average groups show the best performance; the highest dividend-payers and the lowest dividend-payers show slightly inferior performance.

Table 7-1
Stocks Ranked by Dividend Yield

One Year–Close to Close

Statistical Data	Lowest			Middle		Highest	
	1	2	3		4	5	6
Return-Group	23.32	15.03	14.61	15.54	16.25	19.16	17.30
Return-All	16.51	16.51	16.51	16.51	16.51	16.51	16.51
Pct Over	44.67	42.22	41.78	43.45	45.56	44.44	48.67
Beta	1.60	.94	.91	.92	.93	1.18	1.01
Std Err Beta	.17	.11	.10	.02	.07	.07	.07
Std Err Alpha	4.74	2.86	2.60	.54	1.98	2.01	1.99
R Squared	84.13	83.41	84.97	99.25	91.06	94.15	92.26
T Value	9.21	8.97	9.51	45.98	12.76	16.04	13.81
Geom Mean	1.179	1.128	1.127	1.138	1.144	1.164	1.150
Std Dev Group	37.82	22.36	21.35	19.90	21.10	26.38	22.79
Std Err Est	15.98	9.66	8.78	1.83	6.69	6.77	6.73

Composite Measures	1	2	3		4	5	6
Alpha	-3.12	-.54	-.39	.42	.90	-.36	.61
Sharpe Index	.62	.67	.68	.78	.77	.73	.76
Treynor Index	14.56	15.94	16.08	16.98	17.48	16.21	17.11
Down Mkt Index	1.95	.57	.43	-.46	-.97	.30	-.60

Table 7-2
Stocks Ranked by Dividend Yield

Two Years–Close to Close

Statistical Data	Lowest			Middle		Highest	
	1	2	3	3	4	5	6
Return-Group	47.67	33.29	29.81	32.62	33.16	42.05	37.18
Return-All	34.70	34.70	34.70	34.70	34.70	34.70	34.70
Pct Over	45.11	40.67	38.44	39.91	40.44	45.78	45.56
Beta	1.57	.86	.99	.87	.95	1.39	1.07
Std Err Beta	.21	.16	.10	.02	.07	.11	.08
Std Err Alpha	9.64	7.26	4.47	1.08	3.02	5.16	3.67
R Squared	77.29	64.19	86.32	98.83	92.64	90.31	91.66
T Value	7.38	5.36	10.05	36.73	14.19	12.21	13.26
Geom Mean	1.390	1.296	1.261	1.302	1.302	1.365	1.334
Std Dev Group	51.97	31.18	31.06	25.60	28.58	42.63	32.66
Std Err Est	26.27	19.79	12.19	2.94	8.22	14.07	10.00

Composite Measures	1	2	3	3	4	5	6
Alpha	-6.82	3.49	-4.61	2.26	.35	-6.26	-.12
Sharpe Index	.92	1.07	.96	1.27	1.16	.99	1.14
Treynor Index	30.36	38.76	30.06	37.28	35.07	30.20	34.59
Down Mkt Index	4.34	-4.06	4.64	-2.58	-.37	4.50	.11

Table 7-3
Stocks Ranked by Dividend Yield

One Year–Ave High/Low

Statistical Data	*Lowest* 1	2	3	*Middle*	4	*Highest* 5	6
Return-Group	18.76	14.85	14.17	14.01	12.48	13.93	12.69
Return-All	14.29	14.29	14.29	14.29	14.29	14.29	14.29
Pct Over	47.11	47.11	43.33	44.41	43.11	40.67	44.89
Beta	1.48	1.04	1.00	.95	.87	1.02	.99
Std Err Beta	.16	.12	.09	.02	.08	.07	.09
Std Err Alpha	3.10	2.36	1.76	.49	1.65	1.43	1.88
R Squared	84.89	82.82	88.81	98.93	87.18	92.62	87.20
T Value	9.48	8.78	11.27	38.44	10.43	14.17	10.44
Geom Mean	1.165	1.137	1.131	1.132	1.117	1.130	1.117
Std Dev Group	22.18	15.84	14.65	13.18	12.79	14.63	14.60
Std Err Est	9.15	6.96	5.20	1.45	4.86	4.22	5.54
Composite Measures	1	2	3		4	5	6
Alpha	-2.41	-.08	-.13	.43	.11	-.66	-1.43
Sharpe Index	.85	.94	.97	1.06	.98	.95	.87
Treynor Index	12.67	14.21	14.16	14.75	14.42	13.65	12.84
Down Mkt Index	1.63	.08	.13	-.46	-.13	.64	1.45

Comment and Interpretation

The results of this study are not particularly surprising in terms of market risk. One would expect an investment in the lowest group of dividend-yielding stocks (group 1) to result in higher risk because these companies generally had insufficient earnings to pay out in the form of dividends. That is, the majority of these companies earned less than $1 per share and could not pay a satisfactory dividend. On the other hand, the next group of twenty-five stocks with low dividend yields (group 2) experienced a dramatic drop in market risk. For example, using year-end closing prices, while group 1 had a Beta of 1.60, group 2 showed a Beta of only 0.94. This dramatic drop in market risk implies that there is a substantial difference in companies which do not pay a dividend and those paying a nominal dividend. In contrast, the slightly above-average market risk for high-yielding stocks may be somewhat surprising to some income-oriented investors, but generally these high-yielding stocks reflect a situation where dividends exceed earnings, thereby causing high risk.

Neither is it surprising that the total returns of high-yielding stocks generally failed to outperform the market. In this case, the high-yielding stocks represented companies of questionable growth. And as one may expect, the returns of the middle group of stocks, representing those stocks which paid an "average" yield, were less than the market returns.

On a year-by-year analysis, the low-dividend paying group (group 1) showed extraordinarily poor defensive performance. In every one of the seven years in which the market advanced less than 5 percent, this group performed worse than the market. On the other hand, during the eleven years when the market showed a year-to-year gain in excess of 5 percent, this group outperformed the market ten times. The implication of this finding for a security analyst is to favor companies which do not pay a dividend only if the analyst is certain that the overall market will advance. Otherwise, on a risk-adjusted basis, the analyst would be more inclined to favor those stocks in the average-yield group. In this middle group, the stocks outperformed the market five out of the seven years in which the market advanced less than 5 percent, and in each of the other two years—1966 and 1969—the difference in performance was not significant.

As mentioned above, on a risk-adjusted basis, the groups paying the least dividends (groups 1, 2, and 3) tended to show inferior performance. The Alpha statistics of this group over the three time periods were negative eight out of nine times; and the Sharpe Index, Treynor Index, and Down Market Index were consistently worse than the middle group. With regard to the highest-dividend yielding stocks, groups 4, 5, and 6, the results were also slightly inferior when measured on a risk-adjusted basis. In these groups, the Alpha statistic was negative five out of nine times; the Sharpe

Index was inferior in each of the nine possibilities, and the Treynor and Down Market Index were worse than that for the middle group in seven out of nine times. On balance then, on a risk-adjusted basis, the evidence supports the desirability of those equities which have an average or perhaps slightly above-average dividend yield, all other factors being equal.

Conclusion

The above findings do not support either the "primacy of dividends" or the "dividends don't count" theories discussed in the beginning of this chapter. Rather, the evidence in this study supports the position that there is risk/return informational content in the dividend-yield ratio which should be helpful to a security analyst; namely, that high returns and high risk are associated with companies paying little or no dividends (group 1), and that superior risk-adjusted returns can be found in average to slightly above average dividend-yielding stocks. In contrast, inferior risk-adjusted returns were found in stocks paying either low or high dividends, that is, the extremes.

But the flaw in using dividend-yield rather than the payout ratio as a quantitative tool in security analysis is that it does not fully test the commonly held notion that retained earnings should generate higher price appreciation. Whereas the denominator in the yield formula is market price, the denominator in the payout ratio is earnings. This capital-gains phenomenon, in part related to the dividend-yield problem via the numerator, is examined in the next chapter.[a]

---

[a]An example of this phenomenon is IBM, presumably a well-recognized "growth-issue." In 1972 IBM had a low yield (1.5 percent) but a high payout ratio (52 percent). If one hypothesizes that low payout ratios are indicators of high growth, IBM would not qualify; but if one associates low yields with high growth, IBM would qualify.

8

Payout Ratio and Investment Results

While the prior chapter reported on the risk/return relation between the dividend yield and investment results, this chapter considers the risk/return relation between the payout ratio and investment results. As such, these two chapters are complementary. The major conceptual difference is that while the dividend yield is a major consideration of the investor, the payout ratio is more closely identified with a decision by the company.

This chapter first discusses the traditional normative model used in determining payout policy; second, it presents empirical evidence of some prior studies linking the payout ratio to investment results; and third, the findings of this study are discussed. These findings are based on two sets of criteria; first, prior year's earnings are used in the numerator, that is, reported by the company and generally known to the financial community and, second, current year's earnings are used. In this latter case the actual earnings for the prior nine months are generally known, and estimates for the remaining three months are assumed accurate.

The Traditional Models and Theory

In theory, there is a predefined payout ratio which should be acceptable to a shareholder. This value in its loosest and simplest form is the point at which the returns from reinvestment by the company will be equal to that available to the shareholder. If the former exceeds the latter, then the company should retain its earnings; if the latter exceeds the former, then the company should pay out its earnings to its shareholders.

The problem, of course, is not so simple. How can a shareholder's alternative opportunities for reinvestment be known? What is the role of risk? of tax consequences? of dividend stability? What portion of earnings should be retained as a buffer or defensive strategy to preserve the existence of the company? What is the shareholder's discount rate and how does this rate vary over time?

In any case, the payout ratio, computed as the ratio of dividends to earnings, is mathematically related to a company's growth rate as follows:

$$G = R(1 - P) \tag{8.1}$$

$$P = 1 - G/R$$

where: G = growth rate of the firm.

R = rate of return on book value.

P = payout ratio.

In this equation, the growth rate increases inversely to the payout ratio so that the higher the payout ratio, the lower the growth rate. The presumption, then, is that investors will search for those companies that have a high rate of return and a low payout ratio if capital growth is the objective.

Next, consider the relation between the P/E ratio and the payout ratio. By drawing on the classical dividend-valuation model proposed by J.B. Williams[1] we find:

$$V = D/(r - g) \tag{8.2}$$

where: V = justified value or price.

D = expected dividends.

r = discount rate.

g = growth of dividends.

Here we see that the higher the growth rate, the higher the value of the firm; also the higher the expected dividend, the higher the value of the firm.

Now consider Graham, Dodd, and Cottle's argument (see Chapter 4) that the justified price of an equity is some multiple of expected earnings:

$$V = E \times P/E \tag{8.3}$$

where: V = justified value or price.

E = expected earnings.

P/E = price-earnings ratio as some function of growth, quality and so forth (see Chapter 4).

Equating these two values (V) from equations 8.2 and 8.3,

$$\frac{D}{r - g} = E \times P/E$$

and that the payout ratio (D/E) now becomes:

$$D/E = (r - g) \times P/E \tag{8.4}$$

The significance of this simple transformation may be somewhat ambiguous. For example, it is clear mathematically from equation 8.4 that for a given payout ratio and discount rate, any increase in the growth rate must be accompanied by an increase in the P/E ratio. It is also clear that for any given P/E ratio any increase in the growth rate must be offset by a decrease in the payout ratio, all other factors being equal. What is not (intuitively) clear, however, is why the P/E ratio is directly proportional to the payout ratio; that is, the higher the P/E, the higher the payout ratio if r and g are held constant. This direct relationship appears inconsistent with our empirical knowledge of the equity markets where high P/E's generally have low payout ratios.

On further examination of the variables, however, it is clear that one variable cannot be held constant in the equation. For example, if income is retained, that is, lowering the D/E ratio, growth (g) will rise along with P/E. Furthermore, the discount rate (r) is an increasing function of growth (g) since future dividends incur greater risk than near dividends. As a result, we find that D/E need not fluctuate directly with P/E since the remaining variables, r and g, are affected whenever D/E or P/E are changed.

A more useful mathematical formula expressing the relation of the value of a stock to the payout ratio involves the market capitalization rate:[2]

$$V = \frac{D + R(E - D)}{C}$$

where: V = justified value.

   D = dividend.

   R = ratio of the productivity of retained earnings to the market capitalization rate.

   E = earnings.

   C = market capitalization rate, or E/P.

The advantage of using this expression is that whenever R is greater than 1.0, that is, when the returns from reinvestment exceed the average returns from the market, the more desirable it is to retain earnings. Alternatively, if R is small, shareholders can benefit by receiving high dividends for subsequent reinvestment in companies with returns greater than the market capitalization rate.

To summarize, the theoretical framework in determining a payout ratio for a particular company is simply a function of the number and profitability of a company's alternative investments vis-à-vis the shareholder's expected return on his alternative investments. A firm should retain its earnings if its alternatives are numerous and profitable; if restricted and unprofitable, the company (theoretically) should pay out its earnings to its shareholders.

Some Differing Views

Graham et al.

These authors feel that "distributed earnings have had a greater weight in determining market prices than have retained and reinvested earnings."[3] According to these authors, the reason that dividends play a dominant role is that the present worth of near-dividends is higher than that of distant-dividends; therefore, all other factors being equal, the stock of companies paying higher dividends will usually sell at a higher price. While they caution that investors do not expect companies to pay out all of their earnings, they do support their "dividends count" theory by observing that "poor earnings and a good payout may do as well for stockholders as good earnings and a poor payout."[4]

Their case for liberal dividends is further supported by their observations that oftentimes the level of retained earnings is not reflected in the price of the stock. They state that:

If reinvested earnings cannot be depended upon to increase or even to maintain dividends, it is obvious that they cannot be depended upon to reflect themselves in a corresponding increase in the average market price of the shares.[5]

Graham et al., do advise, however, that in the "new theory" involving growth stocks, where the rate of return on reinvestment is higher than the alternative investment by the shareholder, low payout is justified.

Modigliani and Miller

These scholars argue that the division between distributed earnings and retained earnings, that is, the payout ratio, is not particularly important.

As long as management is presumed to be acting in the best interests of the stockholders, retained earnings can be regarded as equivalent to a fully subscribed, pre-emptive issue of common stock. Hence, for present purposes, the division of the stream between cash dividends and retained earnings in any period is a mere detail.[6]

As shown later, Modigliani and Miller's hypothesis is not entirely borne out by the evidence in this author's study.

Prior Studies

M. Nerlove

Nerlove examined the mean retained earnings per dollar of assets as a critical variable in explaining rates of return from common stocks.[7] Nerlove used the COMPUSTAT data base having information on 371 companies over the period 1950-64. Both long- and short-term effects were analyzed by subdividing the fifteen-year longer-term period into three five-year periods.

The results of Nerlove's tests regarding retained earnings were as follows:

1. The most important variables explaining differences among rates of return over both short and long periods are sales growth and retention of earnings.
2. Growth in earnings appears to be of considerably less importance than either growth in sales or retention of earnings.
3. Dividends are of considerably less quantitative significance than retained earnings.

In addition, Nerlove found that retained earnings were even more important when analyzed on an industry-by-industry basis.

But there are several problems in interpreting Nerlove's evidence. First, the role of market risk had not been fully accounted for by Nerlove. He concludes that the higher rates of return found in companies having relatively high retained earnings per dollar of assets are due to market disequilibrium. But how does he know that these higher rates of return do not merely reflect the additional risks involved? By using risk-adjusted measures of performance, as in this author's study, one might find that risk alone accounted for these higher rates of return and not market disequilibrium.

Second, one is always suspect of multiple-regression analysis because of the collinearity of the independent variables. An example of the problems in interpreting Nerlove's findings is that "the coefficient of the rate of growth of earnings is consistently positive and significant in each of the three five-year periods but, surprisingly, fails to emerge as significant in the full-period regressions."[8] While this result may be mathematically correct, it is most difficult both to rationalize this phenomenon and to apply it as a rule of thumb in security analysis.

Finally, while one may conclude from the coefficients in Nerlove's regression equations that retained earnings per asset dollar are important but dividends are not, how does the corporate financier extend this result into his decision process in recommending a dividend-payout policy? Are not dividends and retained earnings so interrelated that, if one ratio is important, must not the other also be important?

In summary, while Nerlove's findings may be mathematically correct, his conclusions must be viewed with caution.

Irwin Friend and Marshall Puckett

Friend and Puckett present empirical evidence on whether or not stockholders are indifferent between current dividends and retained earnings.[9] Their procedure involved first normalizing the earnings-price ratio using time-series regression. This normalized earnings-price ratio was then compared to the payout ratio (D/E) to find whether or not E/P ratios varied with the payout ratio. That is, as reflected in the values of the resulting regression coefficients, did shareholders in fact tend to pay more or less for differing values of payout ratios?

The empirical results reported by Friend and Puckett were somewhat mixed, but they did conclude:

Our analysis suggests that there is little basis for the customary view that in the stock market generally, except for unusual growth stocks, a dollar of dividends has several times the impact on price of a dollar of retained earnings.

. . . It is our opinion that those statistical studies purporting to show strong market preference for dividends are in error.[10]

One of the reasons for these mixed results is the omission of other variables, particularly risk and growth, in their regression equations. Perhaps on a risk-adjusted basis, their conclusions would be different. Another reason is that the regression equations did not distinguish between companies having high earning power from those having relatively low earning power, even though both may have a low payout ratio. For example, in the former the P/E could be high and the payout low due to investor enthusiasm for the company's growth prospects; in the latter case both the P/E and the payout could be low due to a lack of investor enthusiasm and poor growth prospects. As such, in Friend and Puckett's study, these two nonhomogenous groups would be represented as one homogenous group of companies having low payout ratios.

Results—Payout Ratio (Lagged One Year)

Tables 8-1, 8-2 and 8-3 show the results of the study:

1. *Risk*. The market risk of stocks of companies having low payout ratios (groups 1, 2, and 3) is somewhat greater than that of companies with high payout ratios (groups 4, 5, and 6).
2. *Return*. Group 1, the "portfolio" of twenty-five stocks containing the lowest payout ratios, has significantly higher returns than the remaining groups.
3. *Risk-adjusted Results*. On a risk-adjusted basis, the middle group is superior.

Comment and Interpretation

The results appear to be consistent with theory. The stock prices of companies which retained their earnings appreciated more than those of companies which paid out their earnings. If year-end prices are used, the average return of the stocks in group 1 was 24.1 percent compared to an average of 17.3 percent for the entire group (see Table 8-1). The returns found in groups 2 and 3 were likewise superior but not to the degree found in group 1.

In contrast to the high returns found in groups 1, 2, and 3, the average returns of companies which had a high payout ratio, groups 4, 5, and 6, were somewhat lower. While the returns of the former outperformed the averages nine out of nine times, the returns of the latter were lower than the averages nine out of nine times.

But one must also consider market risk. The Beta of the stock group of low payout companies steadily decreased as the payout increased. As seen in Table 8-1, group 1's Beta was 1.49; group 2's, 1.22; and group 3's, 1.15. The same decreasing sequence was gound in the two-year and the average high/low pricing periods. The average Beta for all three groups of low payout-ratio companies for all three pricing periods was 1.27. In contrast, the average Beta for high payout companies for all three pricing periods was only 0.88; moreover, the range of this Beta was consistently low, fluctuating between 0.80 and 0.98.

A year-by-year analysis of group 1 confirms the responsiveness of this group to the market. Group 1 stocks outperformed the market in all but two of the twelve years in which the market advanced. In 1967, for example, this group appreciated 87.7 percent compared to 43.2 percent for the averages; in 1965, this group appreciated 73.1 percent compared to 30.6 percent for the market. But in market downturns, the opposite occurred.

Table 8-1
Stocks Ranked by Payout Ratio, Lagged One Year

One Year–Close to Close

Statistical Data	*Lowest*			*Middle*		*Highest*	
	1	2	3		4	5	6
Return-Group	24.15	18.90	19.90	16.49	15.92	12.89	15.49
Return-All	17.29	17.29	17.29	17.29	17.29	17.29	17.29
Pct Over	47.06	42.59	48.00	43.17	45.41	40.47	41.88
Beta	1.49	1.22	1.15	.91	.85	.82	.89
Std Err Beta	.15	.10	.08	.03	.06	.07	.08
Std Err Alpha	4.13	2.81	2.22	.74	1.54	1.86	2.11
R Squared	87.13	90.75	93.35	98.77	94.13	90.96	90.32
T Value	10.08	12.13	14.51	34.75	15.51	12.28	11.83
Geom Mean	1.193	1.156	1.171	1.147	1.143	1.112	1.136
Std Dev Group	35.12	28.12	26.20	20.27	19.40	18.87	20.67
Std Err Est	13.41	9.11	7.19	2.39	5.00	6.04	6.85

Composite Measures	1	2	3		4	5	6
Alpha	-1.56	-2.11	.04	.69	1.16	-1.22	.08
Sharpe Index	.69	.67	.76	.81	.82	.68	.75
Treynor Index	16.24	15.55	17.33	18.05	18.64	15.79	17.38
Down Mkt Index	1.05	1.74	-.04	-.76	-1.35	1.49	-.09

Table 8-2
Stocks Ranked by Payout Ratio, Lagged One Year

Two Years–Close to Close

Statistical Data	*1*	*Lowest* 2	*3*	*Middle*	*4*	*Highest* 5	*6*
Return-Group	45.83	37.53	38.15	30.97	32.36	26.03	32.03
Return-All	33.22	33.22	33.22	33.22	33.22	33.22	33.22
Pct Over	47.06	40.71	47.76	41.15	41.65	36.47	36.94
Beta	1.50	1.25	1.12	.89	.93	.80	.98
Std Err Beta	.16	.17	.08	.03	.09	.09	.07
Std Err Alpha	7.06	7.47	3.33	1.36	3.90	4.03	2.89
R Squared	85.45	78.45	93.71	98.24	88.05	83.87	93.72
T Value	9.39	7.39	14.95	28.97	10.51	8.83	14.96
Geom Mean	1.381	1.313	1.340	1.285	1.294	1.236	1.288
Std Dev Group	47.37	41.20	33.99	26.29	28.89	25.68	29.52
Std Err Est	19.24	20.37	9.07	3.71	10.63	10.98	7.88
Composite Measures	*1*	*2*	*3*		*4*	*5*	*6*
Alpha	−3.86	−3.89	.80	1.39	1.60	−.65	−.41
Sharpe Index	.97	.91	1.12	1.18	1.12	1.01	1.08
Treynor Index	30.64	30.10	33.93	34.78	34.94	32.40	32.79
Down Mkt Index	2.58	3.12	−.72	−1.57	−1.72	.81	.42

Table 8-3
Stocks Ranked by Payout Ratio, Lagged One Year

One Year-Ave High/Low

Statistical Data	Lowest			Middle	Highest		
	1	2	3		4	5	6
Return-Group	19.75	17.22	17.23	14.40	13.29	10.97	11.54
Return-All	14.67	14.67	14.67	14.67	14.67	14.67	14.67
Pct Over	47.76	48.47	49.41	45.04	40.94	37.65	36.71
Beta	1.33	1.26	1.14	.94	.87	.82	.93
Std Err Beta	.15	.12	.11	.03	.07	.06	.12
Std Err Alpha	3.04	2.46	2.26	.56	1.34	1.23	2.43
R Squared	84.16	87.82	87.40	98.74	92.21	92.51	79.96
T Value	8.93	10.40	10.20	34.33	13.32	13.61	7.74
Geom Mean	1.178	1.156	1.159	1.136	1.125	1.103	1.106
Std Dev Group	20.49	18.91	17.13	13.41	12.84	12.10	14.60
Std Err Est	8.68	7.03	6.47	1.60	3.82	3.53	6.96

Composite Measures	1	2	3		4	5	6
Alpha	.20	-1.20	.57	.54	.46	-1.13	-2.04
Sharpe Index	.96	.91	1.01	1.07	1.03	.91	.79
Treynor Index	14.82	13.72	15.18	15.24	15.20	13.30	12.47
Down Mkt Index	-.15	.96	-.50	-.57	-.53	1.37	2.20

That is, in the five years when the market did not advance, group 1 stocks did worse than the averages in three of these years. Particularly, in the recent years of 1969 and 1970, these stocks declined 20.8 percent and 20.5 percent when the market changed 14.0 percent and 0.0 percent respectively.

On a risk-adjusted basis, the results indicate superior performance of the middle group. The Alphas of this middle group were positive in all three time periods. In addition, the three Sharpe Indexes of the middle group were larger than any of the other eighteen Sharpe Indexes; and the Treynor and Down Market Indexes were superior to the others in all but two of the eighteen pricing periods. According to these results, if one's goal is to outperform the market on a risk-adjusted basis, he should concentrate on investments in companies in this middle group. However, if the investor has perfect foresight regarding the direction of the market, he would invest in the high Beta group, that is, those companies having low payout ratios.

Results—Payout Ratio (Current Year's Earnings)

Whereas the first study did not require any earnings forecasts, this second study requires a certain amount of forecasting. It assumes, for example, that for fiscal year-end companies the earnings are known at year-end while in reality only nine months' earnings are known, and the remaining three months' earnings must be estimated. The objective of this study, then, is to examine any differences in results which may be due to the value of current rather than prior year's earnings. (See Tables 8-4, 8-5 and 8-6 for results.)

Interestingly, the results were not substantially different. In nine out of nine possible cases, the groups of companies having low payout ratios had higher returns than those with high payout ratios. Similarly, the market risk in each of these cases was higher in the low payout groups. In these low payout groups, the Beta fluctuated between 1.49 and 1.12 while that for high payout groups ranged between 0.71 and 1.06. And again the middle group performed the best on a risk-adjusted basis.

The implication of this finding is that the payout ratio can be calculated using data generally available to the financial community. In other words, this evidence indirectly suggests that a company's payout ratio is relatively stable, and for use in security analysis, last year's payout ratio is a reliable estimate for this year's payout ratio.

Conclusion

Companies showing a high payout ratio are indeed suspect. In the majority

Table 8-4
Stocks Ranked by Payout Ratio

One Year–Close to Close

Statistical Data	Lowest			Middle	Highest	
	1	2	3	4	5	6
Return–Group	23.54	19.70	20.92	16.28	13.16	11.13
Return–All	16.51	16.51	16.51	16.51	16.51	16.51
Pct Over	46.67	47.33	49.56	44.65	40.67	39.33
Beta	1.58	1.12	1.20	.91	.77	1.04
Std Err Beta	.14	.10	.07	.02	.05	.07
Std Err Alpha	3.74	2.61	2.04	.46	1.35	1.94
R Squared	89.26	89.55	94.15	99.45	93.69	93.00
T Value	11.53	11.71	16.05	53.76	15.41	14.58
Geom Mean	1.183	1.170	1.181	1.146	1.118	1.086
Std Dev Group	36.27	25.73	26.77	19.80	17.15	23.35
Std Err Est	12.61	8.82	6.87	1.56	4.57	6.55
Composite Measures	1	2	3	4	5	6
Alpha	-2.58	1.14	1.12	-.92	.51	-6.04
Sharpe Index	.65	.77	.78	.68	.77	.48
Treynor Index	14.88	17.53	17.45	15.37	17.18	10.70
Down Mkt Index	1.63	-1.01	-.94	1.14	-.66	5.81

Table 8-5
Stocks Ranked by Payout Ratio

Two Years–Close to Close

Statistical Data	Lowest			Middle	Highest		
	1	2	3		4	5	6
Return-Group	47.40	40.72	41.30	33.59	28.88	25.76	28.91
Return-All	34.70	34.70	34.70	34.70	34.70	34.70	34.70
Pct Over	47.56	43.11	47.33	42.13	37.11	33.56	32.67
Beta	1.49	1.19	1.15	.93	.80	.71	1.00
Std Err Beta	.15	.14	.08	.03	.06	.05	.12
Std Err Alpha	6.60	6.17	3.58	1.13	2.83	2.34	5.23
R Squared	86.66	82.53	92.97	98.85	91.17	92.20	82.44
T Value	10.19	8.69	14.54	37.05	12.86	13.75	8.67
Geom Mean	1.400	1.355	1.371	1.309	1.266	1.240	1.252
Std Dev Group	46.47	37.95	34.69	27.14	24.45	21.54	32.06
Std Err Est	18.00	16.83	9.76	3.09	7.70	6.38	14.25

Composite Measures	1	2	3		4	5	6
Alpha	-4.20	-.40	1.41	1.41	1.04	1.09	-5.80
Sharpe Index	1.02	1.07	1.19	1.24	1.18	1.20	.90
Treynor Index	31.88	34.36	35.92	36.22	35.99	36.23	28.90
Down Mkt Index	2.82	.34	-1.22	-1.52	-1.29	-1.53	5.80

Table 8-6
Stocks Ranked by Payout Ratio

One Year–Ave High/Low

Statistical Data	Lowest			Middle	Highest	
	1	2	3	4	5	6
Return-Group	21.82	21.35	21.11	14.78	8.25	3.39
Return-All	14.29	14.29	14.29	14.29	14.29	14.29
Pct Over	52.89	55.11	56.67	47.68	29.33	22.67
Beta	1.49	1.21	1.23	.92	.85	1.06
Std Err Beta	.13	.12	.10	.02	.06	.09
Std Err Alpha	2.56	2.29	1.97	.48	1.16	1.88
R Squared	89.38	87.39	90.62	98.91	93.07	88.64
T Value	11.61	10.53	12.44	38.09	14.66	11.17
Geom Mean	1.197	1.199	1.197	1.140	1.075	1.022
Std Dev Group	21.80	17.91	17.90	12.81	12.21	15.50
Std Err Est	7.53	6.74	5.81	1.42	3.41	5.54

Composite Measures	1	2	3	4	5	6
Alpha	.47	4.01	3.46	1.58	-3.95	-11.73
Sharpe Index	1.00	1.19	1.18	1.15	.68	.22
Treynor Index	14.61	17.60	17.10	16.01	9.78	3.21
Down Mkt Index	-.32	-3.30	-2.80	-1.72	4.63	11.09

of cases it is evident that too high a payout simply foretells an investor that insufficient funds are being set aside by the company for asset replacement. The results show a decidedly inferior return on an investment in these companies.

On the other hand, companies showing a low payout ratio are also suspect for they appear to generate an excessive amount of market risk. While the returns of this group are high, the risk is also high. As a result, on a risk-adjusted basis, the performance appears inferior. In conclusion, therefore, only the middle group shows evidence of a superior risk-adjusted return.

Finally, the evidence presented here can be considered a refinement of prior studies on the payout ratio. The most important refinement is the treatment of risk. For example, while Nerlove's findings that growth of retained earnings is a variable which is associated with market disequilibrium, the evidence presented here suggests that it is more closely associated with market risk. With regard to the Friend and Puckett study, the evidence presented in this chapter supports their conclusion that "those statistical studies purporting to show strong market preference for dividends are in error." That is, as shown here, one may have a strong market preference for a company with a high payout ratio only if he is willing to be satisfied with lower returns *and* lower risk. This finding, like Friend and Puckett's, questions those studies which indicate investor preference for dividends without regard for risk.

But now let us consider the effect of dividend changes on the risk/return aspects of investments.

9

**Dividend Changes and
Investment Results**

This chapter presents evidence on the risks and returns of investments in
common stocks of companies which have changed their dividend rate. The
criterion for ranking is the percentage increase or decrease in dividends
paid per share in the year of analysis relative to that paid in the prior year.
For example, most of the companies in groups 1 and 2 have lowered their
dividends while the companies in groups 5 and 6 have shown the largest
increase in dividends. The companies in the middle had largely left their
dividend rate unchanged.

The Controversy

The controversy whether or not dividends are important was discussed in
Chapter 7. It was pointed out that two schools of thought dominate; one
school arguing that dividends are the main determinant of stock prices and
the other that "dividends don't count." This chapter extends this
controversy by examining not the absolute value of dividends, nor the
yield, nor the relative payouts, as in Chapters 7 and 8, but whether or not a
change in the dividend rate is important.

In this respect, dividend increases can affect shareholders in one of two
ways. First, any increase in dividends would benefit the shareholders
simply because the shareholder values present dividends higher than future
ones. If one argues that the worth of a stock is the present value of all
discounted dividends, then cash dividends received today are worth more
than the same dividend received sometime in the future. Therefore one may
conclude that a dividend increase is beneficial to the shareholder.
Moreover, one can further argue that risk is similarly reduced because
present cash is in the control of the shareholder and (presumably) less risky
than that if retained by the firm for reinvestment in some project unknown
to the shareholder.

On the other hand, the shareholder may be adversely affected by any
dividend increase since the company would have fewer internal funds
available to it for additional expansion, thereby requiring the firm either to
forego possible growth or to seek external financing. If this external
financing involves the issuance of new shares, then, according to the
"dividends don't count" school (see Chapter 7), the value of the new

shares equals the decreased value of the firm's shares; and in this case the net economic result of raising the dividend is nil.

Prior Studies

Myron J. Gordon

Gordon examined the relationship between common stock prices and (1) both the dividends and earnings, (2) dividends only, and (3) earnings only.[1] Using the cross-sectional rather than the time-series approach, Gordon regressed price, dividend, and earnings of 164 companies in four industries (chemicals, foods, steel, and machine tools) in each of two years, 1951 and 1954.

Since this chapter is concerned only with dividend growth, a discussion of Gordon's findings is restricted here to this one variable. In this respect, Gordon argues that retained earnings is "the most important and predictable cause of growth in a corporation's dividend."[2] Therefore, in Gordon's regression of price against dividends and retained earnings, it is the coefficient of the retained earnings variable which is important since it reflects dividend growth. His hypothesis, then, is that if dividend increases are important in equity valuations, this coefficient should be positive.

The empirical findings of Gordon's study were described by him as "particularly disturbing" since these coefficients turned out quite low, and in fact were negative for the chemical industry in 1954. The rationale for these low coefficients for dividend growth is that if investors value growth highly, then any increase in dividends will lower retained earnings and the company's growth prospects would correspondingly be diminished.

But one of the problems in the above study is that retained earnings was used as a proxy for dividend growth. Gordon properly points out that "a model in which it is possible to use the rate of growth itself might yield better results."[3] Accordingly, Gordon proposes another model which defines dividend growth as the difference between current dividend and the average dividend for the prior five years, each deflated by book value. Using this model, Gordon finds that the coefficients for the average five-year dividend are greater than those for dividend growth, that is, current year's dividend minus the average five-year dividend. Gordon's interpretation of this higher coefficient is that "investors adjust to a change in dividend with a lag."[4] And for purposes of this study, it is this lag which is of interest to us. If a lag does exist, capital markets are not as efficient as the random walk hypothesis would suggest.

Results—Dividend Changes

The evidence presented in Tables 9-1, 9-2, and 9-3 suggests that:

1. *Risk*. Market risk is slightly higher for investments in companies which have substantially changed their dividends from the prior year; this change can be either an increase or a decrease.
2. *Return*. Higher returns are found in stocks of companies which increased their dividends.
3. *Risk-adjusted Results*. Lower risk-adjusted returns are found in stocks of companies which decreased their dividends. Superior risk-adjusted returns are found in groups 4 and 5, the companies which declared only moderate increases in their dividend rate.

Comment and Interpretation

The results of this study show that dividend changes are important. Most interesting is the decidedly inferior returns of group 1, the group containing companies which decreased their dividends. The Alpha risk-adjusted returns of this group were consistently negative; and the Sharpe, Treynor and Down Market Indexes all indicated inferior returns.

In the two time periods where performance was measured from year-end to year-end, in the first case over one year and in the second case over two years, not only was the return of group 1 stocks generally lower than the other groups but market risk was (slightly) higher. And these results occurred when all the information necessary for decision-making was completely known. That is, the dividend decrease had already been reported before year-end and the price of the stock was known at the time of investment.

Also, note the substantially inferior performance of group 1 when the average high/low price of the stock is used. This inferior performance is not unexpected because not all the information is known at the time of investment. For example, the high of the high/low price may have occurred before the announcement of the dividend cut, which subsequently caused a sharp decline in the price of the stock. The implications to an investor are clearly to avoid companies which have either reported or are expected to report a decline in their dividend rate, a conclusion perhaps obvious to a practicing investor but not at all clear to those who argue that "dividends don't count."

The second interesting statistic in this analysis is that group 5, the group containing the twenty-five stocks reporting only moderate increases in

Table 9-1
Stocks Ranked by Dividend Changes

One Year—Close to Close

Statistical Data	Lowest			Middle	Highest		
	1	2	3		4	5	6
Return-Group	15.77	14.92	16.54	15.41	20.15	21.09	19.53
Return-All	17.29	17.29	17.29	17.29	17.29	17.29	17.29
Pct Over	41.18	41.88	39.76	42.61	48.47	51.06	46.12
Beta	1.09	.86	1.11	.86	1.02	1.02	1.16
Std Err Beta	.06	.06	.08	.04	.07	.09	.07
Std Err Alpha	1.68	1.58	2.12	1.04	2.07	2.57	2.05
R Squared	95.63	93.94	93.50	97.24	92.76	89.18	94.38
T Value	18.12	15.25	14.69	23.01	13.86	11.12	15.87
Geom Mean	1.132	1.133	1.138	1.138	1.179	1.188	1.166
Std Dev Group	24.48	19.55	25.39	19.12	23.44	23.84	26.34
Std Err Est	5.45	5.12	6.89	3.36	6.71	8.35	6.65

Composite Measures	1	2	3		4	5	6
Alpha	-3.01	.06	-2.72	.62	2.45	3.44	-.54
Sharpe Index	.64	.76	.65	.81	.86	.88	.74
Treynor Index	14.52	17.36	14.85	18.01	19.68	20.66	16.82
Down Mkt Index	2.77	-.07	2.44	-.72	-2.39	-3.37	.47

Table 9-2
Stocks Ranked by Dividend Changes

Two Years—Close to Close

Statistical Data	Lowest			Middle	Highest		
	1	2	3		4	5	6
Return-Group	33.79	29.26	34.42	29.03	35.90	39.75	38.86
Return-All	33.22	33.22	33.22	33.22	33.22	33.22	33.22
Pct Over	38.35	39.76	43.06	39.29	44.47	47.29	42.35
Beta	1.18	.96	1.14	.84	1.09	.97	1.15
Std Err Beta	.10	.08	.09	.04	.11	.10	.11
Std Err Alpha	4.41	3.70	3.97	1.68	4.96	4.32	4.90
R Squared	90.30	89.76	91.44	97.00	86.27	86.77	87.72
T Value	11.82	11.47	12.66	22.02	9.71	9.92	10.35
Geom Mean	1.291	1.258	1.304	1.267	1.320	1.365	1.341
Std Dev Group	36.22	29.61	34.76	24.89	34.25	30.38	35.79
Std Err Est	12.01	10.09	10.83	4.59	13.51	11.77	13.35

Composite Measures	1	2	3		4	5	6
Alpha	-5.28	-2.58	-3.30	1.21	-.21	7.63	.82
Sharpe Index	.93	.99	.99	1.17	1.05	1.31	1.09
Treynor Index	28.73	30.53	30.31	34.66	33.03	41.11	33.93
Down Mkt Index	4.49	2.69	2.91	-1.44	.19	-7.90	-.71

Table 9-3
Stocks Ranked by Dividend Changes

One Year-Ave High/Low

Statistical Data		*Lowest*		*Middle*		*Highest*	
	1	*2*	*3*		*4*	*5*	*6*
Return-Group	7.61	11.21	12.49	13.09	19.07	21.11	21.40
Return-All	14.67	14.67	14.67	14.67	14.67	14.67	14.67
Pct Over	29.88	37.18	37.65	42.21	58.59	55.53	56.24
Beta	1.06	.94	1.06	.91	.96	.95	1.18
Std Err Beta	.10	.09	.11	.04	.10	.10	.11
Std Err Alpha	2.13	1.87	2.23	.73	1.97	2.09	2.23
R Squared	87.33	87.38	86.26	97.68	86.91	85.13	88.57
T Value	10.17	10.19	9.70	25.14	9.98	9.27	10.78
Geom Mean	1.063	1.103	1.113	1.123	1.182	1.202	1.201
Std Dev Group	16.05	14.12	16.17	12.95	14.60	14.53	17.72
Std Err Est	6.08	5.34	6.30	2.10	5.62	5.97	6.38

Composite Measures	*1*	*2*	*3*		*4*	*5*	*6*
Alpha	-7.98	-2.52	-3.12	-.22	4.92	7.17	4.06
Sharpe Index	.47	.79	.77	1.01	1.31	1.45	1.21
Treynor Index	7.16	11.98	11.74	14.43	19.77	22.21	18.10
Down Mkt Index	7.51	2.69	2.93	.24	-5.10	-7.54	-3.43

dividends, outperformed group 6, the group reporting the largest increase. This result, however, is not particularly surprising since many of the companies in group 6 merely reinstated dividend cuts made in prior years. For example, Kroehler Manufacturing cut their dividend in 1967 from $1.00 to $.26; then raised their dividend in 1968 to $.60; then back to $1.00 in 1969. A company with such an erratic dividend record in this study would be assigned to group 6, but it would be of questionable character in reflecting dividend growth. In contrast, companies in group 5 tended to be less erratic in changing their dividend rate.

Conclusion

The empirical findings presented in this chapter suggest that changes in the dividend rate are important. On a risk-adjusted basis, the stocks of companies which decreased their dividend rate were generally inferior to those which have maintained or increased their dividend rate. And the stocks of companies which had moderately, but not excessively, increased their dividend rate appear to be the superior performers on a risk-adjusted basis.

Let us now reflect on the relation between size, as measured by total invested capital, and investment results.

10 Total Invested Capital and Investment Results

Typically, an investor or financial analyst hypothesizes that the stock of a smaller company is purchased for capital returns, with its accompanying high risk, and the stock of a larger company is purchased for its safety of principal and, in many cases, its higher yield. The purpose of this chapter is to present risk and return evidence which may support the superiority of one group over the other on a risk-adjusted basis. The hypothesis, as before, is that the market is in fact in equilibrium and that the size of a company is not in any way indicative of either superior or inferior risk-adjusted performance.

Prior Studies

To this author's knowledge, there are no published reports linking size as measured by the total invested capital and investment results. However, there are two related studies which indirectly bear on the evidence presented in this study. These are, in turn, one by I.M.D. Little who examined the relation between asset size and growth rates, and one by R.M. Sedgwick who studied the relation between market value and common stock returns.

I.M.D. Little

Little's main purpose in studying growth rates was to find out whether or not there was any correlation between future and past growth rates of a company. That is, in his words, "Does growth breed growth"?[1] However, as a corollary to this main purpose, Little also examined the effect of asset size on growth rates; and it is this corollary which is of present interest.

Little's data included 441 large British firms and covered the period 1951-59. Using cross-sectional regression analysis, Little found no significant relation between growth rates and asset size, a finding somewhat at variance with the commonly held notion that as size increases, growth decreases.

This evidence is relevant to this study because it implies that if growth rates are invariant to size, even though highly correlated with capital appreciation, there should be no apparent reason to suspect that the risks and returns of investments in smaller companies would be superior to that in larger companies. As such, Little's evidence lends more support to the hypothesis that historic information is of little value in forecasting the risks and returns of a particular equity. That is, if the underlying growth-rate generating process is random, and if investment results are highly dependent on these growth rates, then it follows that investment results would tend to be random. And if size is independent of earnings growth, then an investor should be indifferent to size in selecting stocks.

R. Minturn Sedgwick

Sedgwick examined the relation of company size and investment results, but used market value of the company's stock as the measure of size rather than total invested capital as in this study.[2] Sedgwick assumed "that a fund is invested in the 20 largest industrial companies in proportion to their size as measured by the total market value of the common stock of each."[3] The results of this investment were then compared to that of 24 "distinguished" investment companies and 36 college endowment funds over the period 1948-72. His findings were as follows:

Not one of the 24 investment companies did as well as either the "20 largest" or the industrial market. In fact, $1,000 in the "20 largest" with dividends reinvested grew about 86 percent more than it would have in a composite of the 24 mutual funds.[4]

In brief, out of 60 large funds of different types—many directed by the most highly paid and eminent managers in the investment community—only one did better than the "20 largest" for a brief ten years.[5]

Sedgwick's results are most interesting because they are contrary to the commonly held view that large companies are held for safety rather than for superior returns. Unfortunately, Sedgwick does not adjust for risk, but after an examination of the stocks held in his "20 largest," one suspects that high market value is indeed a relevant statistic which could result in superior risk-adjusted performance. This result is further discussed in the ensuing section, after presenting the empirical findings of this author's study.

Results—Total Invested Capital

The evidence on this measure is presented in Tables 10-1, 10-2, and 10-3.

1. *Risk.* The market risk of groups 1 and 2, the fifty companies with the

Table 10-1
Stocks Ranked by Total Invested Capital

One Year—Close to Close

Statistical Data	Lowest			Middle		Highest	
	1	2	3		4	5	6
Return-Group	24.53	18.82	19.74	16.29	12.65	12.68	12.13
Return-All	16.51	16.51	16.51	16.51	16.51	16.51	16.51
Pct Over	51.33	44.67	47.11	44.19	39.56	38.44	39.33
Beta	1.32	1.16	.97	1.02	.85	.88	.79
Std Err Beta	.14	.09	.07	.02	.06	.06	.09
Std Err Alpha	3.73	2.43	1.92	.44	1.67	1.77	2.51
R Squared	85.30	91.38	92.24	99.60	92.37	91.93	82.28
T Value	9.63	13.02	13.79	63.05	13.92	13.50	8.62
Geom Mean	1.207	1.159	1.178	1.143	1.111	1.110	1.106
Std Dev Group	30.97	26.30	21.96	22.05	19.24	19.81	18.98
Std Err Est	12.59	8.19	6.49	1.48	5.64	5.97	8.47

Composite Measures

	1	2	3		4	5	6
Alpha	2.73	-.34	3.66	-.49	-1.45	-1.79	-.99
Sharpe Index	.79	.72	.90	.74	.66	-.79	.64
Treynor Index	18.58	16.22	20.27	16.03	14.81	14.46	15.27
Down Mkt Index	-2.07	.30	-3.76	.48	1.70	2.05	1.25

Table 10-2
Stocks Ranked by Total Invested Capital

Two Years–Close to Close

Statistical Data	Lowest			Middle		Highest	
	1	2	3		4	5	6
Return-Group	51.58	39.08	42.64	34.27	25.92	26.54	25.14
Return-All	34.70	34.70	34.70	34.70	34.70	34.70	34.70
Pct Over	49.11	44.44	48.67	41.67	33.11	31.33	36.22
Beta	1.37	1.17	.87	1.01	.82	.92	.84
Std Err Beta	.14	.13	.09	.02	.06	.08	.12
Std Err Alpha	6.36	5.75	3.94	.80	2.91	3.72	5.54
R Squared	85.65	84.09	86.19	99.51	90.97	88.75	74.47
T Value	9.77	9.20	9.99	57.16	12.70	11.23	6.83
Geom Mean	1.455	1.342	1.400	1.311	1.236	1.236	1.223
Std Dev Group	43.11	37.05	27.26	29.35	24.92	28.50	28.18
Std Err Est	17.32	15.67	10.74	2.17	7.94	10.14	15.10

Composite Measures	1	2	3		4	5	6
Alpha	3.99	−1.44	12.46	−.65	−2.42	−5.48	−3.86
Sharpe Index	1.20	1.05	1.56	1.17	1.04	.93	.89
Treynor Index	37.61	33.46	49.03	34.05	31.74	28.76	30.08
Down Mkt Index	−2.91	1.24	−14.33	.65	2.96	5.94	4.62

Table 10-3
Stocks Ranked by Total Invested Capital

One Year–Ave High/Low

Statistical Data	Lowest 1	2	3	Middle	Highest 4	5	6
Return-Group	20.91	16.48	16.35	13.98	11.05	10.71	10.88
Return-All	14.29	14.29	14.29	14.29	14.29	14.29	14.29
Pct Over	51.33	49.11	48.89	43.51	41.56	37.78	40.89
Beta	1.20	1.12	.91	1.03	.89	.93	.86
Std Err Beta	.14	.11	.09	.02	.08	.07	.12
Std Err Alpha	2.73	2.15	1.72	.49	1.51	1.44	2.33
R Squared	82.65	87.08	87.43	99.07	89.47	91.17	77.00
T Value	8.73	10.38	10.55	41.29	11.66	12.86	7.32
Geom Mean	1.195	1.152	1.156	1.131	1.103	1.099	1.101
Std Dev Group	18.22	16.60	13.47	14.23	12.96	13.46	13.51
Std Err Est	8.05	6.33	5.06	1.46	4.46	4.24	6.87

Composite Measures	1	2	3		4	5	6
Alpha	3.75	.43	3.31	-.69	-1.65	-2.61	-1.40
Sharpe Index	1.15	.99	1.21	.98	.85	.80	.81
Treynor Index	17.42	14.68	17.92	13.63	12.44	11.49	12.66
Down Mkt Index	-3.12	-.39	-3.62	.67	1.86	2.80	1.63

lowest total invested capital, is relatively high. The middle group shows about average market risk, and the largest companies U (groups 4, 5, and 6) contain relatively low market risk.

2. *Return*. Substantially higher returns are found in groups 1, 2, and 3, the seventy-five companies having the lowest total invested capital; in contrast, significantly lower returns are found in groups 4, 5, and 6, the seventy-five companies having the largest amounts of invested capital; and the middle groups show about average returns.

3. *Risk-adjusted Results*. Superior risk-adjusted returns are found in investments in the smaller companies; and within the smaller companies, the best risk-adjusted returns are contained in group 3, the companies ranked between fifty-one and seventy-five rather than in groups 1 and 2.

Comment and Interpretation

The results of this study do confirm one's general impression that an investment in large firms is less risky than one in smaller companies. What is somewhat surprising is the substantial decrease in market risk as one progresses from groups 1 and 2 to group 3. That is, the first fifty ranked companies with the smallest amounts of total invested capital had high Betas. But group 3, containing the companies ranked between fifty-one and seventy-five, had below-average Betas. At the same time, this group showed only a slight decrease in the rate of return.

On a risk-adjusted basis, it is seen that small companies usually outperform large companies. The evidence shows that in all three pricing periods the Alphas were positive in the three low-capital groups (groups 1, 2, and 3) in seven out of nine times. In contrast, the Alphas in the high-capital groups (groups 1, 2, and 3) were negative nine out of nine times. The other three risk-adjusted measures, the Sharpe, Treynor, and Down Market Index, indicated similar results. (A note of caution, however, is necessary in interpreting these findings for one must not think that these results would necessarily apply to small companies not included in the S & P 425; rather, these results apply only to fairly well established companies such as those found in the S & P 425.)

Also impressive is the consistency with which the smaller companies outperformed the larger ones. First impressions of the returns could suggest that a few small firms may have contributed a disproportionate amount of appreciation while the remainder did not necessarily perform well. This lack of consistency of the smaller groups was not the case; that is, the percentage of the number of stocks in each of the three lowest groups and in each of the three pricing periods was higher in all nine cases compared to their counterparts in groups 4, 5, and 6.

The role of bias in this particular study is subject to debate. On the one hand, before being presented with the evidence in this chapter, one can argue that large firms should by definition show superior returns. That is, it is "obvious" that the firms comprising the S & P 425 index as of year-end 1971 will show superior performance since these are the successful, well-financed firms that have survived over the past twenty years. On the other hand, it is also "obvious" to other observers that the smaller firms should show superior performance because this group represents the successful smaller firm which has risen in value over the past twenty years and has subsequently achieved a position in the S & P 425 list of established companies. Accordingly, some caution is necessary in interpreting the evidence presented in this chapter.

With regard to the findings of Sedgwick that superior returns are found in investments of companies having high market value, the evidence presented here is not necessarily in conflict with his findings. The reason is simply that this study used total invested capital as a measure of a company's size while Sedgwick used total market value. This difference could be most relevant since companies with high total invested capital are not necessarily the same as those with high market value. While the former would contain the stable, nongrowth company, the latter could contain the high P/E growth-type company.

Conclusion

The evidence here indicates that superior risk-adjusted returns can be found in the low-capital companies comprising the S & P 425. While the first two groups of twenty-five stocks showed both high returns and high risk, the third group showed above-average returns at a substantially decreased market risk. Large companies consistently showed low returns and low risk, a finding perhaps not inconsistent with expectations.

This chapter considered only total invested capital; let us now look at the return on this total invested capital.

11 Rate of Return on Invested Capital and Investment Results

Rate-of-return analysis is oftentimes used to evaluate a firm's alternative investment opportunities. In theory, if the firm's rate of return on an investment project exceeds its cost of capital, the firm should undertake the investment; if not, the investment should be avoided.

The concern in this study is whether or not a firm's historic rate of return on total invested capital is related at all to stock price returns. On the one hand the financial analyst can argue that high historic rates of return are leading indicators of future growth, for as more funds are employed in capital projects by the company, higher earnings result. Accordingly, capital gains accrue to the investors who purchase equities in these high rate-of-return companies.

On the other hand, a financial analyst can argue that prices of equities in low rate-of-return companies are generally undervalued and therefore offer the highest potential for appreciation. They argue that in an economy characterized by competition, rates of return should find levels which tend to be substantially equal for all firms, after adjusting for risk, liquidity, and other factors. If each firm does in fact have equal opportunities to achieve this given rate of return, then low rates of return generally increase and high rates of return generally decrease as competitive forces evolve. The problem here, however, is that capital already invested is not easily converted into alternative investment projects, and that rates of return are not particularly quick to respond to competitive forces.

In any case, one would suspect that a high rate of return connotes "good management" and that a low rate of return implies "inferior management." But these suspicions are much too vague to be useful to the financial analyst. What the financial analyst needs is some indication of the risk/return characteristics of companies which report high rates of return compared to those reporting low rates of return.

Prior Studies

Robert P. Colin

Colin, director of research at Faulkner, Dawkins & Sullivan (FDS), a

NYSE investment firm, presents data showing the superiority of firms having a high earnings rate of return.[1] In his study using Compustat data, Colin found that an investment in companies which reported a high earnings return substantially outperformed an investment in the market indexes. More specifically, during the period 1958 to 1971, Colin shows that the returns, unadjusted for risk, of investments in companies having a high earnings rate of return was about twice as great as that of the average stock in the Compustat universe.

The rationale for using rate of return as a key ratio in investment analysis is explained by Colin:

The preference of this firm [FDS] and its research group is to concentrate its efforts in high rate of return industries and companies. The simplistic rationale for this approach is as follows: Given the consistency of rate of return on equity, it is arithmetically correct that a high rate of return company will record growth at a faster rate than a low rate of return company.

[Therefore], it would seem that a proper analytical and investment approach is to place a major proportion of resources within this universe. This is the intention of the F.D.&S. Research Group.[2]

In later reports, Colin uses computer screening techniques to select companies having a high five-year average rate of return on total capitalization, but then adds other growth requirements, including a superior five-year and latest twelve-month earnings growth-rate record.

Results—Rate of Return

Tables 11-1, 11-2, and 11-3 present the evidence:

1. *Risk.* Companies reporting low rates of return in earnings show relatively high market risk.
2. *Returns.* Slightly higher returns are found in companies reporting low rates of return in earnings.
3. *Risk-adjusted Results.* Higher risk-adjusted returns are associated with companies showing high rates of return in earnings.

Comment and Interpretation

While it is not surprising that the market risk of companies reporting low rates of return was relatively high, it is surprising that inferior returns were associated with companies reporting high rates of return. As such, these results are not consistent with those reported by Robert Colin. The cause of

Table 11-1

Stocks Ranked by Rate of Return on Invested Capital

One Year–Close to Close

Statistical Data	Lowest			Middle	Highest		
	1	2	3		4	5	6
Return-Group	20.87	21.37	18.50	15.35	16.56	17.60	19.26
Return-All	17.29	17.29	17.29	17.29	17.29	17.29	17.29
Pct Over	45.88	50.59	44.94	41.31	42.82	46.82	48.71
Beta	1.23	1.20	1.09	.94	.89	.83	.89
Std Err Beta	.11	.09	.08	.02	.07	.09	.09
Std Err Alpha	3.03	2.65	2.31	.56	2.01	2.63	2.48
R Squared	89.68	91.45	92.08	99.32	91.20	83.82	86.99
T Value	11.42	12.67	13.20	46.97	12.47	8.82	10.02
Geom Mean	1.175	1.183	1.158	1.135	1.147	1.159	1.175
Std Dev Group	28.74	27.62	25.04	20.83	20.61	19.96	20.97
Std Err Est	9.83	8.60	7.50	1.82	6.51	8.55	8.05

Composite Measures	1	2	3		4	5	6
Alpha	-.48	.65	-.35	-.93	1.12	3.27	3.92
Sharpe Index	.73	.77	.74	.74	.80	.88	.92
Treynor Index	16.90	17.83	16.97	16.30	18.55	21.23	21.71
Down Mkt Index	.39	-.55	.32	.99	-1.26	-3.94	-4.42

Table 11-2
Stocks Ranked by Rate of Return on Invested Capital

Two Years–Close to Close

Statistical Data	Lowest			Middle	Highest		
	1	2	3		4	5	6
Return-Group	46.25	35.42	33.88	29.31	32.20	34.03	36.74
Return-All	33.22	33.22	33.22	33.22	33.22	33.22	33.22
Pct Over	45.41	44.71	40.71	38.60	42.59	44.71	47.29
Beta	1.31	1.06	1.05	.95	.88	.86	.81
Std Err Beta	.16	.10	.08	.02	.10	.09	.14
Std Err Alpha	7.13	4.23	3.33	.83	4.41	4.17	6.06
R Squared	81.45	89.15	92.89	99.41	83.97	84.65	70.09
T Value	8.12	11.10	14.00	50.28	8.86	9.10	5.93
Geom Mean	1.404	1.315	1.301	1.265	1.293	1.315	1.340
Std Dev Group	42.38	32.87	32.01	27.78	28.23	27.23	28.37
Std Err Est	19.43	11.53	9.09	2.27	12.03	11.36	16.52
Composite Measures	1	2	3		4	5	6
Alpha	2.84	.20	-1.13	-2.13	2.84	5.59	9.78
Sharpe Index	1.09	1.08	1.06	1.05	1.14	1.25	1.29
Treynor Index	35.39	33.41	32.14	30.97	36.43	39.75	45.27
Down Mkt Index	-2.17	-.19	1.08	2.25	-3.21	-6.54	-12.06

Table 11-3
Stocks Ranked by Rate of Return on Invested Capital

One Year-Ave High/Low

Statistical Data	Lowest			Middle	Highest		
	1	2	3		4	5	6
Return-Group	16.36	17.26	14.67	13.25	14.90	15.28	17.64
Return-All	14.67	14.67	14.67	14.67	14.67	14.67	14.67
Pct Over	43.76	48.24	44.94	41.40	46.12	47.29	53.41
Beta	1.09	1.19	1.03	.97	.97	.84	.87
Std Err Beta	.15	.13	.09	.02	.07	.09	.12
Std Err Alpha	3.04	2.69	1.79	.42	1.38	1.75	2.52
R Squared	77.84	84.31	90.16	99.34	93.21	86.45	76.79
T Value	7.26	8.98	11.72	47.34	14.35	9.78	7.05
Geom Mean	1.150	1.157	1.136	1.124	1.140	1.146	1.168
Std Dev Group	17.36	18.22	15.33	13.76	14.18	12.78	14.06
Std Err Est	8.70	7.68	5.12	1.19	3.93	5.01	7.21

Composite Measures	1	2	3		4	5	6
Alpha	.44	-.13	-.46	-1.01	.67	2.93	4.83
Sharpe Index	.94	.95	.96	.96	1.05	1.20	1.25
Treynor Index	15.07	14.56	14.23	13.63	15.36	18.14	20.20
Down Mkt Index	-.40	.11	.44	1.04	-.69	-3.47	-5.53

difference between the results presented in this chapter and those reported by Colin is the sample composition. While this study focused on the stocks in the S & P 425 Index, Colin used a universe of about 1,800 stocks.

In any respect, on a risk-adjusted basis, the evidence here is consistent with the commonly-held view that high rates of return are preferable to low rates of return. All four measures of risk-adjusted results (Alpha, Sharpe, Treynor, and Down Market Indexes) indicated superior performance of stocks associated with companies reporting high rates of return. For example, on a year-to-year basis, Table 11-1, the Alphas of groups 1, 2, and 3, that is, stocks ranked 1 to 75, were −0.48, 0.65, and −0.35. In contrast, the Alphas for groups 4, 5, and 6, that is, the seventy-five companies with the highest rates of return, were 1.12, 3.27, and 3.92. This superiority was also found using the average high/low price, Table 11-3, as well as the closing prices over a two-year period, Table 11-2.

Conclusion

The results confirm the commonly held notion that superior risk-adjusted results are found in companies reporting relatively high rates of return on total invested capital. This superiority, however, resulted from their comparatively low market risk rather than from their high market returns. Because of this latter finding, analysts who favor companies with low rates of return during market upswings appear to be correct.

12 Debt/Capital Ratio and Investment Results

The impact of debt on the market value of a firm is most controversial. One view is that, except for tax consequences, the capital structure of firms in the same risk class has no effect on a firm's market valuation, assuming market equilibrium.[1] In contrast, the traditional view is that some debt affords an opportunity for earnings leverage and higher market valuation but that too much debt reduces the market value of the firm because of the additional risks involved. According to this traditional view, there is an "optimum" debt/equity ratio which will maximize the market value of the firm.

But there are two separate decisionmakers involved in this controversy: first, the potential investor or security analyst who makes decisions on the value of a particular equity and, second, the corporation's management who makes decisions on the incremental returns from the proposed use of additional funds. In this second case, for example, traditionalists may argue that a debt-free firm can raise the price of its stock by incurring more debt and reinvesting these funds at a rate higher than the firm's cost of capital. This argument presumes an incremental analysis, requiring data on the expected return from the proposed use of the funds. Unfortunately, however, the investor or security analyst seldom has the necessary data to evaluate this particular management decision.

Therefore the problem posed to the investor or security analyst is to judge the risks and returns from alternative strategies, given some range of debt/capital ratios available to him from many companies. Should he invest in companies with high debt/capital ratios, or low ones? As such, this chapter presents evidence on the historic relation between debt/capital ratios and risk-adjusted returns. Rather than assuming market equilibrium, as required in the controversial arguments involving the impact of debt on the market value of a firm, this chapter presents evidence on the possible existence of market disequilibrium.

Prior Studies

Modigliani and Miller

Modigliani and Miller cite two examples to support their argument that the debt/equity ratio does not affect market valuation or the cost of capital.[2] These two examples involve forty-three large electric utilities and forty-two oil companies, using average figures for the years 1947 and 1948 in the former and figures for 1958 in the latter. In correlating the capitalization rate and the debt/equity ratio, MM found that the two were not significantly related. In their words:

The results of these tests are clearly favorable to our hypothesis. Both correlation coefficients are very close to zero and are not statistically significant. Furthermore, the implications of the traditional view fail to be supported even with respect to the sign of the correlation. The data in short provide no evidence of any tendency for the cost of capital to fall as the debt ratio increases.[3]

Note, however, that this empirical evidence does not necessarily support their assumption regarding market equilibrium. That is, the fact that the capitalization rate is not correlated to the debt/equity ratio does not necessarily imply that superior risk-adjusted returns cannot be found in one debt/capital value over another.

H. Benishay

Benishay used cross-sectional multiple regression analysis on the data of fifty-six companies in the years 1954-57 and found a negative relationship between the debt/equity ratio and the capitalization rate.[4] This finding did not support his original hypothesis that "we should expect a positive sign for the debt-equity coefficient (i.e., the higher the debt, the larger the risk of default, the less valuable the equity and the larger the rate of return)."[5]

But in interpreting his findings, Benishay suggests that as the debt/equity ratio becomes larger, it becomes a proxy for size; that is, the higher the ratio, the larger the company. Therefore the investor appears willing to accept a lower rate of return for increased size and more safety, a finding consistent with this author's study. In this regard, Benishay concludes:

The debt-equity ratio relationship shows inconclusive results difficult to interpret unequivocally. Although in all four cross-sections its coefficients are negative, it is unwarranted to conclude that a high debt-equity ratio is an indicator of a desirable characteristic, since in the context of this study the debt-equity ratio could be mainly a measure of size thereby obliterating its use as a measure of risk.[6]

One of the reasons Benishay's study is referred to here is to reemphasize the difficulties in using cross-sectional multiregression techniques (see Chapter 3). When introducing many variables into an equation, the resulting coefficients become difficult to interpret due to the collinearity of the independent variables. Furthermore, as discussed in Chapter 3, it is not at all clear that the resulting coefficients are time invariant.

William P. O'Connor, Jr.

O'Connor, partner in the firm, Moore & Schley, Cameron & Co., uses case studies of some ten companies and the chemical industry to illustrate that debt is a "quality defect."[7] In his analysis, as a practitioner in security analysis, he argues:

Although business school students are taught that the stockholder should benefit when borrowed money is used to increase the assets working for him, the record shows that most of the time long-term debt is bad for stockholders.[8]

One problem with O'Connor's case analysis is that it identifies only companies which have experienced excess capacity, and in times of market downturns, the stock of such a company has not been particularly profitable for shareholders. This observation by O'Connor is borne out by the evidence presented in this study, that is, that the stock of a highly leveraged company generally does not do well in market downturns. However, a different story emerges in market upturns since highly leveraged firms perform rather well. But in support of O'Connor's view that debt is "bad for shareholders," the evidence does indicate slightly inferior risk-adjusted returns for companies that are highly leveraged.

Results—Debt/Capital Ratio

The evidence presented in Tables 12-1, 12-2, and 12-3 indicates the following:

1. *Risk.* The stock of a highly leveraged company contains more market risk than that of a company with a low debt/capital ratio.
2. *Return.* The returns of stocks of companies with high debt/capital structures are slightly higher than those of their counterparts.
3. *Risk-adjusted Results.* Slightly superior risk-adjusted returns are found in companies having low debt/capital ratios.

Comment and Interpretation

The evidence presented in this study supports the generally accepted

Table 12-1
Stocks Ranked by Debt/Capital

One Year—Close to Close

Statistical Data	Lowest		Middle		Highest	
	1	2	3	4	5	6
Return-Group	15.51	18.83	14.49	16.75	19.00	19.44
Return-All	16.51	16.51	16.51	16.51	16.51	16.51
Pct Over	42.67	48.67	41.11	41.78	44.89	47.56
Beta	.91	.84	.86	1.04	1.26	1.17
Std Err Beta	.08	.07	.07	.07	.10	.07
Std Err Alpha	2.15	1.85	1.87	2.00	2.81	1.97
R Squared	89.31	90.44	90.67	92.64	90.35	94.21
T Value	11.56	12.30	12.47	14.19	12.24	16.14
Geom Mean	1.137	1.173	1.129	1.144	1.157	1.166
Std Dev Group	20.89	19.02	19.49	23.46	28.81	26.06
Std Err Est	7.24	6.24	6.32	6.75	9.49	6.65

Composite Measures	1	2	3	4	5	6
Alpha	.47	5.04	.34	-.46	-1.87	.16
Sharpe Index	.74	.99	.74	.71	.66	.75
Treynor Index	17.02	22.54	16.91	16.07	15.03	16.65
Down Mkt Index	-.51	-6.03	-.40	.44	1.48	-.14

Table 12-2
Stocks Ranked by Debt/Capital

Two Years—Close to Close

Statistical Data	Lowest			Middle	Highest		
	1	2	3		4	5	6
Return-Group	33.08	36.42	31.88	33.46	37.08	37.33	44.46
Return-All	34.70	34.70	34.70	34.70	34.70	34.70	34.70
Pct Over	40.89	44.22	41.33	39.92	41.11	43.78	45.11
Beta	.92	.79	.83	1.00	.93	1.22	1.29
Std Err Beta	.12	.07	.07	.02	.11	.11	.12
Std Err Alpha	5.54	3.01	3.13	1.04	4.88	4.90	5.36
R Squared	77.96	89.94	89.94	99.16	82.38	88.82	88.15
T Value	7.52	11.96	11.96	43.37	8.65	11.27	10.91
Geom Mean	1.300	1.344	1.295	1.304	1.338	1.322	1.391
Std Dev Group	30.32	24.38	25.36	29.18	29.88	37.64	39.98
Std Err Est	15.09	8.20	8.53	2.84	13.30	13.35	14.60

Composite Measures	1	2	3		4	5	6
Alpha	1.15	8.84	3.19	-1.19	4.73	-4.98	-.31
Sharpe Index	1.09	1.49	1.26	1.15	1.24	.99	1.11
Treynor Index	35.95	45.82	38.56	33.51	39.78	30.61	34.46
Down Mkt Index	-1.25	-11.12	-3.86	1.19	-5.08	4.09	.24

Table 12-3
Stocks Ranked by Debt/Capital

One Year-Ave High/Low

Statistical Data		*Lowest*		*Middle*		*Highest*	
	1	2	3	4	5	6
Return-Group	14.36	17.15	12.00	13.80	13.62	16.57
Return-All	14.29	14.29	14.29	14.29	14.29	14.29
Pct Over	47.56	50.44	41.78	42.86	44.22	48.00
Beta	.83	.92	.90	.98	1.09	1.33
Std Err Beta	.08	.07	.08	.02	.09	.11
Std Err Alpha	1.66	1.44	1.53	.30	1.80	2.11
R Squared	85.89	91.02	89.45	99.62	90.16	90.76
T Value	9.87	12.74	11.64	64.70	12.11	12.54
Geom Mean	1.137	1.164	1.112	1.130	1.124	1.148
Std Dev Grou	12.31	13.33	13.08	13.58	15.90	19.29
Std Err Est	4.90	4.24	4.51	.89	5.29	6.22
Composite Measures	1	2	3	4	5	6
Alpha	2.54	3.98	-.81	-.24	-2.02	-2.47
Sharpe Index	1.17	1.29	.92	1.02	.86	.86
Treynor Index	17.36	18.61	13.39	14.05	12.45	12.44
Down Mkt Index	-3.07	-4.32	.91	.24	1.84	1.85

notion that for industrial companies, high debt/capital ratios imply high market risk. This finding is not surprising because as a firm takes on more debt it is faced with higher interest costs. Since these fixed interest costs are insensitive to economic downturns, they cause the highly leveraged companies to incur lower earnings and price instability. As expected, in market upturns these stocks generally outperform the market and in downturns they usually decline more than the market.

The evidence in this regard is rather consistent as far as market risk is concerned. The Beta statistics are summarized below for the three twenty-five-stock groups having low debt/capital ratios as well as for the three twenty-five-stock groups having high debt/capital ratios:

	Beta Statistics					
Pricing Period	Low Debt/Capital Groups			High Debt/Capital Groups		
	1	2	3	4	5	6
One Year—Close to Close	0.91	0.84	0.86	1.04	1.26	1.17
Two Years—Close to Close	0.92	0.79	0.83	0.93	1.22	1.29
One Year—Average High/Low	0.83	0.92	0.90	1.11	1.09	1.33

From the above it is clear that low debt/capital ratios are indicators of low market risk, and vice versa.

With respect to returns, higher returns are found in the higher leveraged companies. Combining all three pricing periods, the returns from groups 4, 5, and 6 (the three groups of twenty-five companies having the highest debt/capital ratios) were higher than the averages in eight out of nine possible times; and the returns from groups 1, 2, and 3 (the groups of twenty-five companies having the lowest debt/capital ratios) were higher than the averages in only four of the nine times.

On a risk-adjusted basis, the evidence favors investments in companies having low debt/capital ratios. This finding supports O'Connor's observations that debt is, in fact, a "quality defect" and is inherently "bad for stockholders." Note that on a risk-adjusted basis, the Alpha is positive eight out of nine times for companies with low debt/capital ratios and negative seven out of nine times for compamies having high debt/capital ratios. This finding is also supported by the three other risk-adjusted measures, the Sharpe, Treynor, and Down Market indexes, which generally show superior values in groups 1, 2, and 3 compared to those in groups 4, 5, and 6. Interestingly, the middle group shows inferior risk-adjusted returns in all three pricing periods. Therefore, if this evidence does imply inferior risk-adjusted performance of the middle group, one becomes suspect of the traditional view that an investment in a company having neither excessive debt nor one not partaking in the advantages of leverage is an inferior investment. Perhaps, contrary to the advice of Graham et al., it is the middle group which an investor should avoid.

Relationship between This Study and the Modigliani-Miller (MM) Debt/Equity Controversy

Point of View. The purpose of the debate between the MM hypothesis and the traditionalists is to provide some type of guideline or normative model in a firm's decision regarding long-term financing. In contrast, the purpose of this study is to provide evidence for use by an investor and security analyst on the relation between debt/capital ratios and investment results. This evidence is relevant to the firm only if decisionmakers at the firm use it to argue for or against a particular debt/capital structure, recognizing that (1) the middle groups have historically given (slightly) inferior risk-adjusted returns to the shareholders and (2) high debt/capital ratios generally imply high market risk.

Market Efficiency. One of the basic assumptions in the MM model is that the market is in equilibrium; that is, the markets are assumed to be a fluid mechanism which allows funds to flow (frictionless) from over- to under-valued securities. In contrast, it is this very basic assumption which this study is examining.

Risk. MM's theorem is relevant for debt/capital structures of homogeneous risk classes. This study reverses this process by presenting risk evidence for various values of debt/capital ratios.

In summary, then, the evidence presented here indicates some variance between the assumptions in both the MM proposition and the traditionalist view, and the fact that inferior risk-adjusted returns are found in the middle groups while superior risk-adjusted returns are found in the low debt/capital groups.

Conclusion

The evidence presented here suggests that superior returns, unadjusted for risk, can be obtained from highly leveraged companies but that market risk associated with these returns is rather high. For the more conservative investor, low market risk is found among stocks of companies having low debt/capital ratios.

The most surprising evidence presented in this chapter, and also perhaps the most controversial, is that stocks in the middle group had inferior risk-adjusted returns. Not only does this finding suggest market disequilibrium but it also questions the assumptions of the MM hypothesis, the traditionalists, and the rules of thumb proposed by writers on "investment principles"; and it is the validity of these rules of thumb which is of primary importance in this study.

Evidence has been presented now on a wide range of commonly used ratios and measures, including P/E ratios, growth rates, Graham's valuation formula, dividend yields, payout ratios, dividend changes, total invested capital, rate of return, and debt/capital ratios. Let us now summarize these results.

13 Summary of Evidence

The *Beta* (market risk), the *return,* and the *Alpha* (risk-adjusted return) are summarized by group number in Tables 13-1, 13-2, and 13-3 for each financial ratio listed in Chapters 4 to 12.

As discussed in Chapter 3, group 1 contains the twenty-five companies having the lowest value of the particular ratio or measure studied; group 2 includes the twenty-five companies with the second-lowest values, that is, those ranked 26 to 50; and group 3 comprises the third-lowest group of twenty-five companies, that is, those ranked 51 to 75. In the same way, in the section identified as "Highest," group 6 contains the twenty-five companies with the highest value of the particular ratio; group 5, the second-highest; and group 4, the third-highest. For example, in the latter three groups, in the case where data are available for all 425 companies, group 6 would include companies ranked 401 to 425; group 5, from 376 to 400; and group 4, from 351 to 375. The middle group contains companies between group 3 and group 4.

Note that these summary tables are provided only for Betas, returns, and Alphas. Other statistics, such as the standard errors of Beta and Alpha, coefficients of determination, standard errors of estimate, standard deviations, and so forth, are not summarized here even though they are considered important in this study.

Also, with regard to the statistics of the four composite measures of risk-adjusted returns, i.e., Alpha, Sharpe, Treynor, and Down Market Indexes, only Alpha is summarized. The reason for selecting Alpha is not to minimize the conceptual advantages of the other three measures but to recognize the increasing acceptance of Alpha over the others. In any case, a perusal of the four statistical measures shows that they are in fact highly correlated.

Note also that the data for the one-year pricing period rather than either the average high/low or the two-year period are summarized. The data on these later two time periods are not summarized here for two reasons. First, with regard to the average high/low price, the results could be misleading in cases where a high or low price occurs before a company makes its earnings figures available to the public. Such a situation would violate the presumption that all information is known with certainty before an investment is made. Second, with regard to the two-year period, the

129

Table 13-1
Summary of Betas

Ratio or Measure	Lowest 1	2	3	Group Number Middle	4	Highest 5	6
P/E Ratio	1.27	1.13	1.10	.97	.82	.85	.86
P/E Ratio-Earnings Increase	1.17	1.00	.97	.91	.78	.90	.80
Earnings Increase	1.13	1.09	.86	.89	.96	.99	1.27
Earnings Growth (4-year)	1.17	.99	.89	.87	.90	1.20	1.23
Graham's Valuation	1.21	1.19	.94	.89	.82	.95	1.11
Dividend Yield	1.60	.94	.91	.92	.93	1.18	1.01
Payout Ratio	1.58	1.12	1.20	.91	.81	.77	1.04
Payout Ratio (Lagged One Year)	1.49	1.22	1.15	.91	.85	.82	.89
Dividend Changes	1.09	.86	1.11	.86	1.02	1.02	1.16
Total Invested Capital	1.32	1.16	.97	1.02	.85	.88	.79
Rate of Return on Capital	1.23	1.20	1.09	.94	.89	.83	.89
Debt/Capital Ratio	.91	.84	.86	.99	1.04	1.26	1.17

Table 13-2
Summary of Returns

Ratio or Measure	S & P 425 Universe	Group Number						
		Lowest			Middle	Highest		
		1	2	3		4	5	6
P/E Ratio	17.3	23.2	18.7	19.9	17.1	11.5	14.2	15.8
P/E Ratio-Earnings Increase	14.8	19.1	14.9	17.9	13.3	13.4	11.5	16.7
Earnings Increase	14.8	14.0	15.0	13.2	13.9	16.0	13.7	18.4
Earnings Growth (4-Year)	14.5	14.1	11.4	12.8	13.3	15.9	16.1	17.0
Graham's Valuation	14.5	19.5	17.6	16.3	13.5	9.9	10.8	12.7
Dividend Yield	16.5	23.3	15.0	14.6	15.5	16.2	19.2	17.3
Payout Ratio	16.5	23.5	19.7	20.9	16.3	12.4	13.2	11.1
Payout Ratio (Lagged One Year)	17.3	24.2	18.9	19.9	16.5	15.9	12.9	15.5
Dividend Changes	17.3	15.8	14.9	16.5	15.4	20.1	21.1	19.5
Total Invested Capital	16.5	24.5	18.8	19.7	16.3	12.6	12.7	12.1
Rate of Return on Capital	17.3	20.9	21.4	18.5	15.4	16.6	17.6	19.3
Debt/Capital Ratio	16.5	15.5	18.8	14.5	16.0	16.8	19.0	19.4

Table 13-3
Summary of Alphas

Ratio or Measure	Group Number					
	Lowest				Highest	
	1	2	3	4	5	6
P/E Ratio	1.35	−.83	.92	−2.64	−.44	.89
P/E Ratio-Earnings Increase	1.78	.05	3.57	1.88	−1.78	4.91
Earnings Increase	−2.74	−1.14	.44	1.79	−.95	−.41
Earnings Growth (4-Year)	−2.78	−2.89	−.13	2.90	−1.26	−.85
Graham's Valuation	2.01	.32	2.68	−1.92	−2.96	−3.38
Dividend Yield	−3.12	−.54	−.39	.90	−.36	.61
Payout Ratio	−2.58	1.14	1.12	−.92	.51	−6.04
Payout Ratio (Lagged One Year)	−1.56	−2.11	−.04	1.16	−1.22	.08
Dividend Changes	−3.01	.06	−2.72	2.45	3.44	.54
Total Invested Capital	2.73	−.34	3.66	−1.45	−1.79	−.99
Rate of Return on Capital	−.48	.65	−.35	1.12	3.27	3.92
Debt/Capital Ratio	.47	5.04	.34	.46	−1.87	.16

Middle

results need not be summarized because they are very similar to those for the one-year period. As pointed out in Chapter 3, the main purpose of computing returns over both one-year and two-year periods was to insure consistency. It could happen that due to some erratic or unusual occurrence the closing price of a particular issue was not representative of its "normal" price. But, in retrospect, since the results of the one- and two-year periods were similar, this second computation may not have been necessary.

Summary of Risk (Beta)

High market risk was associated with the following indicators:

1. Low P/E ratios.
2. Extremely high earnings growth and extremely low earnings growth.
3. Extremely "undervalued" and extremely "overvalued" situations, as defined by Graham's growth versus P/E criterion.
4. Low (group 1) dividend yields.
5. Low payout ratios.
6. Changes, either increasing or decreasing, in a company's dividend rate.
7. Relatively small total invested capital.
8. Low rates of return on total invested capital.
9. High debt/capital ratios.

Summary of Returns

High returns were associated with:

1. Low P/E ratios.
2. Companies showing the highest growth rate (group 6).
3. "Undervalued" stocks, as defined by Graham's P/E versus growth criterion.
4. Low (group 1) dividend yields.
5. Low payout ratios.
6. Dividend increases.
7. Relatively small total invested capital.
8. Low rates of return on total invested capital (except those in group 6).
9. High debt/capital ratios.

Summary of Risk-Adjusted Returns (Alpha)

Superior risk-adjusted returns were associated with:

1. For P/E ratios, the results were inconclusive.
2. Average and slightly above-average earnings growth; significantly inferior results were found in the low-growth groups.
3. "Undervalued" situations, as defined by Graham's P/E versus growth criterion.
4. Average and slightly above-average dividend yields.
5. Average payout ratios.
6. Moderate dividend increases.
7. Smaller companies, as measured by total invested capital.
8. High rates of return on total capital.
9. Low debt/capital ratios.

Range of Risk-Adjusted Returns (Alpha)

The risk-adjusted returns, as measured by the Alpha statistic, ranged from −6.04 for an investment in companies with a high payout ratio, group 6, to 5.04 for an investment in companies with a relatively low debt/capital ratio, group 2. Figure 13-1 shows this range with the characteristic line of the payout ratio as the upper line and that for the debt/capital ratio on the bottom line. It is only when the market appreciates 55.4 percent per year do these lines intersect. Accordingly, on a risk-adjusted basis and given no market forecast, the evidence suggests that a portfolio manager should favor companies with a relatively low debt/capital ratio and disfavor those showing a high payout ratio. In between these two characteristic lines are values of Alphas for the remaining ratios.

A note of caution is appropriate here. This range of characteristic lines is important only if one assumes that the market cannot be forecast. Alternatively, if one is willing to forecast the market, he should favor values of ratios associated with high Betas if expecting an upturn and, if required to hold equities, he should favor values of ratios associated with low Betas if forecasting a downturn.

Another note of caution here relates to the reliability of these Alphas. For the two extreme cases plotted in Figure 13-1, the standard error of Alpha for the debt/capital ratio was 1.85 and that for the payout ratio was 1.94.

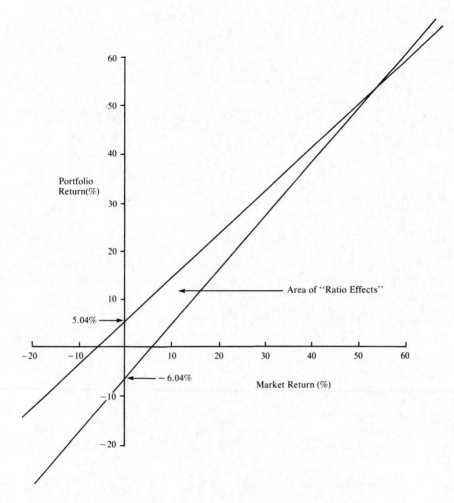

Figure 13-1. Range of Risk-Adjusted Returns

Comment

From these data it is clear that one conclusion of this study is that certain financial ratios and measures are indeed linked to the risks, returns, and risk-adjusted returns from common stocks. But before discussing this conclusion in Chapter 15, let us first give some thought to the implications of this finding on portfolio management. These thoughts are presented in the next chapter.

14

The Principle of Strategy Before Selection

Security analysis has undergone at least three different phases. In the first phase, book value and dividend yield were of primary importance, a phase which lasted until the basic concepts of J.B. Williams (1938) were presented. At that time the basic emphasis shifted, at least in academic circles, to the present value concept. The crux of this second phase was that the value of a common stock was simply the present worth of its future dividend income stream. Arguments immediately arose whether or not the proper variable to be discounted should be dividends, earnings, or dividends and earnings plus some terminal market value; and other arguments involved the proper discount rate to use. The third phase of security analysis took form in the 1950s and 1960s emphasizing earnings and some multiple of earnings; this multiple depended on a company's growth rate, quality of earnings, management, and so forth. This so-called modern method in Graham's words was "a considerable departure from the basic concept of J.B. Williams."[1]

The view presented in this study is that we are now entering a fourth stage, an era of testing and hypothesizing. In this fourth stage, it does appear that different types of stocks respond in different ways to different market conditions.

It follows then that to achieve superior performance an investor or portfolio manager must identify the proper strategies to use at the proper time. This task is not easy, and it requires inputs from specialists in economics as well as security analysts. But the point here is that knowing the risk/return relation of different groups of stocks as presented in this study,and given a market strategy, the portfolio manager is in a position to discuss the merits of individual companies within the framework of the recommended market strategy.

Procedure

Strategy before selection simply means that decision rules regarding the purchase of a particular issue should be made before the security is selected for purchase. While this procedure appears "obvious" to many practitioners, the fact is that very few use such a procedure. The reason for not using this decision-rule approach is that it is not well known how different values

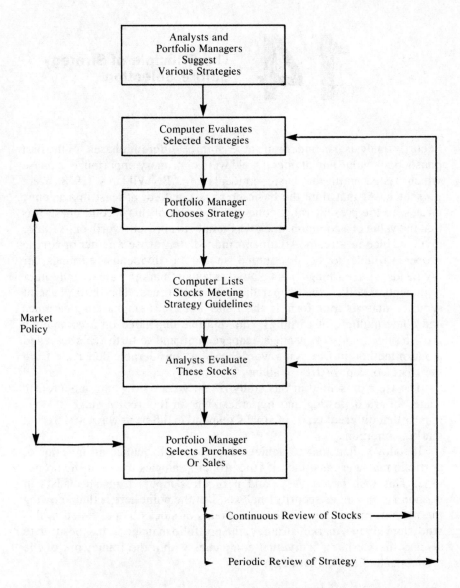

Figure 14-1. Flowchart Procedure for Implementing the Principle of
Strategy before Selection

of different ratios are linked to risks and returns from common stocks; and
it is not at all clear how a portfolio can be structured along these lines.

An overview of a proposed procedure implementing the concept of
strategy before selection is found in Figure 14-1. Consider the following
steps:

Step 1. Analysts and portfolio managers suggest different strategies to be tested in terms of risks, returns, and risk-adjusted returns. These strategies are based on various financial ratios or combinations thereof such as those presented in this study.

Step 2. Next, with the aid of a computer, these risks, returns, and risk-adjusted returns are evaluated for each strategy.

Step 3. Depending on a particular portfolio's risk/return objectives, the portfolio manager chooses a strategy.

Step 4. Stocks meeting the specifications of the strategy are listed by the computer.

Step 5. From the list of stocks in step 4, research analysts identify (subjectively) the less-desirable issues.

Step 6. The portfolio manager selects stocks from this list, since these stocks now meet both the risk/return constraints of the portfolio as well as the approval of the analysts.

As shown by the feedback loops in the diagram, the role of the portfolio manager is most important for he is responsible for choosing both a strategy and the stock of a company which meets the specifications of the strategy. But this strategy must be consistent with market policy; if market policy is positive, then ratios linked with high Betas are preferred; if negative, and if required to hold equities, then ratios linked with low Betas are preferred.

Also note in this strategy-before-selection concept, the stocks purchased by the portfolio manager are continually reviewed by research analysts and monitored by the computer to insure that they meet the specifications of the strategy. (For example, in this latter instance involving a low P/E strategy, a previously noted low P/E stock would be "flagged" by the computer if it attained a high P/E status.) Also note in the feedback loops, the strategy being used is evaluated from time to time in terms of risks, returns, and risk-adjusted returns.

Conclusion

In conclusion, as evidence becomes available that stock prices are indeed linked to the value of one or more financial ratios, it is incumbent upon the portfolio manager to use this information in his professional duties as a money manager. Strategy before selection is a procedure which can be useful in carrying out these duties; and its roots lie in the answers to two questions, first, "Which strategy"? and second, "Which stock"?

15 Conclusions

This study began in Chapter 1 with a statement of the hypothesis and related issues; it will now conclude with a statement of how the evidence presented in this study relates to the hypothesis and related issues. Other conclusions relating to specific ratios are found in each individual chapter discussing the particular ratio.

But before concluding, let us review the steps involved in presenting the evidence. First, a measuring technique was discussed. This measuring technique embodied risk/return concepts currently gaining recognition in so-called modern portfolio theory; it was shown that this same technique can be used in security analysis to measure the risk/return characteristics associated with various financial ratios. In this sense, the validity of the measuring technique is perhaps the most critical element in this study.

Second, data were obtained in computer readable format, and the computer was programmed by the author, thereby transforming the raw data into a form consistent with the aforementioned measuring technique. These data included the necessary information used to calculate certain predefined financial ratios and related stock prices on each of the 425 industrial companies comprising the S & P 425 Index over the twenty-year period 1952-71.

Third, a few financial ratios or measures were selected for testing. These ratios or measures, selected because of their popularity with practicing security analysts and various writers on principles of security analysis, included the price-earnings ratio, earnings growth, Graham's valuation formula, dividend yield, payout ratio, dividend changes, rate of return, total invested capital, and the debt to capital ratio. Each chapter discussed each ratio, including (1) the views of some current writers of textbooks on security analysis, (2) the findings of other researchers regarding the particular ratio, (3) the findings of this study as they relate to risk, return and risk-adjusted return, and (4) some concluding remarks.

Fourth, the data for the one-year period were summarized in Chapter 13 as they reflect (1) market risk (Beta), (2) return, and (3) risk-adjusted return (Alpha). It was at this point that it became evident that certain financial ratios or measures were important in security analysis. And, fifth, because of the importance of the informational value of these ratios, the principle of strategy before selection was presented.

This chapter, then, follows with the conclusions. In presenting these

141

conclusions, both the hypothesis and the six related issues identified in Chapter 1 are examined.

The Hypothesis—Revisited

The hypothesis of this study, as stated in Chapter 1, is

that certain commonly used financial measures or ratios generally known to the financial community have no inherent value in determining risk-adjusted returns from common stocks. This hypothesis, if true, suggests that stock prices are determined only by future events, thereby supporting both the broad form of the random-walk hypothesis and its related efficiency of the marketplace.

For the most part, the evidence presented in this study does not fully support this hypothesis. On a risk-adjusted basis, there does appear to be certain ratio values which are consistently related to superior risk-adjusted returns (Alpha). These risk-adjusted returns, summarized in Table 13-3, range between −6.04 percent and 5.04 percent per year, a difference sufficiently large to question the validity of the broad (semistrong) form of the random-walk hypothesis.

In the same context it also appears that certain values of financial ratios and measures are closely related to both risk and return, that is, as a two-parameter problem. As shown in Tables 13-1 and 13-2, values of Betas and returns are surprisingly consistent. For example, with regard to the debt/capital ratio, the three groups of twenty-five stock portfolios comprising equities of companies with low debt/capital ratios show consistently low Betas, 0.91, 0.84, and 0.86; alternatively, that for high debt/capital ratios are consistently above average at 1.04, 1.26, and 1.17. As such, certain values of financial ratios are not only useful in identifying equities related to superior risk-adjusted returns but are also useful in categorizing issues which may result in high risks and returns, depending on one's ability to forecast the overall market correctly. It is in this context that the principle of strategy before selection, described in the prior chapter, is important.

But the end purpose of this study, as stated in Chapter 1, is "to help portfolio managers and security analysts appraise the risks and rewards of investments in common stocks and to guide them in allocating their time and efforts toward achieving superior results." This end purpose has been accomplished in this study.

Related Issue Number 1—The Dual Nature of Risk and Return

Many studies have been presented in recent years on "systems" which outperform the market. Most of these "systems" show extraordinarily high returns if they had been used in an ex post context, but few of these studies include proper adjustments for risk. If adjusted for risk, much of the evidence presented in recent literature supporting these "systems" is misleading. For example, perhaps the most widely tested ratio is that low P/E stocks generally outperform high P/E stocks. What fails to be mentioned in many of these studies, however, is that low P/E stocks generally contain more market risk than high P/E stocks; accordingly, on a risk-adjusted basis, the superiority of low P/E stocks is not quite so evident.

What is required, then, is an analysis of the relation of varying values of different financial measures using risk-adjusted returns. It is this adjustment which transforms the measuring process from a two-parameter problem, that is, risk and return, to a one-parameter problem, that is, risk-adjusted returns. In this regard, four risk-adjusted measures were used in this study, namely, Alpha, Sharpe, Treynor, and Down Market Indexes. In the end, however, while only Alpha was summarized, the other three measures were found to be highly correlated with Alpha.

With respect to risk, the Beta statistic was found to be useful. Other measures, including the percentage of the number of stocks which outperformed the averages and the standard deviation of each group, were calculated but these measures were not as meaningful as the Beta statistic, primarily because of the latter's linkage to overall market movements.

Also, unique risk, defined as the standard error of estimate as returns of the "portfolio" are regressed against the returns of the market, was not as meaningful as originally presumed. The reason is that these figures were not too consistent from group to group, so that it became difficult to generalize on the relation between unique risk and the particular ratio being tested. There were a few exceptions to this observation, for example, high P/E stocks contain more unique risk than low P/E stocks, but for the most part these statistics were neither consistently high nor low.

Finally, these data do support the basic assumption in portfolio theory that risk is, in fact, directly correlated with return. With few exceptions, high risk was accompanied by high return, and vice versa. To find otherwise would have been a major setback to the development of a rational pricing mechanism in the securities market.

Related Issue Number 2—Fact versus Fiction in Security
Analysis

Textbooks on security analysis typically have a chapter or two on the use of financial ratios in security analysis. But much of the discussion in these chapters usually involves generalities and, in some books, case studies. While not minimizing the importance of generalities and case studies in teaching security analysis, it is also useful to teach relationships. If guidelines can be formulated which show how data generally known to the financial community can be transformed into more meaningful statements regarding a security's return, then these guidelines—along with the evidence supporting the reliability of these guidelines—should be made explicit. Furthermore, the measuring process, together with the evidence used in the measuring process, should be debated and refined by the student himself since there is still much to be learned about the underlying process of price-making in the securities markets.

Related Issue Number 3—The Design of an Information
System for Security Analysts

It was stated in Chapter 1 "that the information-gathering system of a security analyst or portfolio manager should be designed depending on the validity of the random-walk hypothesis." It was seen that the design of this system depended on whether future prices were determined by (1) future events only; (2) historic events, both quantitative and qualitative; or (3) historic events, quantitative only. (Note that the random-walk hypothesis presumes that only future events are relevant.)

In case 1, where future prices are determined by future events only, the information-gathering system depends largely on the amount and quality of private or inside information. Analysts in this group have little use for financial ratios and public information. As such, the evidence in this study does not fully support this approach.

But this approach cannot be treated lightly. For example, in bankruptcy cases and in fraud, financial ratios calculated from misleading and erroneous raw data is of little importance. (One is reminded of the Penn Central bankruptcy and the Equity Funding cases as illustrations of the importance of valid inside information.) In this case, the analyst's dilemma is whether or not valid inside information can be obtained legally and used by him in recommending the purchase or sale of a particular issue.[a]

---

[a]According to the inside information rule, material information obtained surreptitiously from nonpublic sources cannot be used to the investors' advantage. Under this rule, analysts can use nonpublic information in their decision process as long as the information is not material,

In summary then, case 1 presents a most distressing approach to security analysis. If only nonpublic information is relevant to future prices, but its use is illegal, then the job of the analyst in attaining superior performance is indeed difficult, if not impossible.

Case 2 suggests that if past events generally known to the financial community determine future prices, then the analyst must identify which events are important and weight them accordingly. This information may be either qualitative and/or quantitative. If qualitative, the information system must include some knowledge of management and other intangible aspects of the company being analyzed. If both qualitative and quantitative, the system must include not only the above, but also some knowledge of the relation between publicly available data and stock prices. The evidence presented in this study supports this approach.

Consider the research department of a large financial institution. Typically, the analyst assembles substantial amounts of information about a company and its industry while economists provide macroeconomic forecasts to aid the analyst. In assembling this information, the analyst develops an overall impression of the company he is analyzing and a "feel" for the price of the stock. This information is put together so that all the many fragments and diverse elements are blended together to form an integrated picture or "model" of the company, noting that some of the fragments of information typically come from nonpublic as well as public sources. It is this integration of public and nonpublic information which is the basis for the principle of strategy before selection proposed in Chapter 14.

The subtle point here is that the use of financial ratios should play a more important role in security analysis than is generally the case. These financial ratios do help in defining the risks and returns associated with the common stock of different companies and should be used, not automatically, but with caution.

Case 3 suggests that if future prices are highly related to quantitative information, then the analyst must rely on quantitative methods such as man/machine interactive systems and computer screens to achieve superior results. Indeed, after considering the evidence of the historical performance of various investment advisors and portfolio managers, many observers are willing to relegate the decision-making entirely to the computer. While such a system may, in fact, give results equal to man-made decision processes, there is no evidence as yet to support such a procedure. To date, it is generally recognized that while portfolio

that is, if the release of the information will not result in an immediate substantial change in the price of the stock. Otherwise, the analyst is in violation of the rule and subject to action by the New York Stock Exchange and the Securities Exchange Commission. In effect then, the analyst is admonished for performing his analytical and investigative work too well even though acting in the best interests of his clients.

management is becoming more and more of a science, security analysis is still an art.

Related Issue Number 4—Generating an "Efficient Portfolio"

The central issue in the capital asset pricing model and portfolio theory revolves around the trade-off between risk and return. That is, under rationale decision-making, one prefers more return to less return and less risk to more risk. Underlying this theory is the emergence of Beta as the single most important characteristic.

This study presents evidence on risk and return in two dimensions; first as it affects the security analyst and, second, as it relates to the portfolio manager. With regard to the security analyst, it is his job to select securities which will result in above average rates of return at a given risk level. In the context of the performance measures used in this study, the analyst's goals are to recommend stocks yielding positive Alphas. But in his quest for positive Alphas he must be continually cognizant of his assumed risk levels, Betas. Therefore, as an aid in his recommendations of various companies, the analyst should be aware of the risk/return relation between financial ratios and common stocks, the subject of this study.

Second, in his quest to maximize return and minimize risk, the portfolio manager should be continually aware that the strategy of the account is usually more important than the selection of individual securities. For example, whether a portfolio is structured along low (or high) price-earnings ratios is most important; and this decision must precede a decision regarding which security to purchase or sell. The evidence presented in this study confirms the importance of this strategy decision and helps the portfolio manager to structure his portfolios along the "efficient frontier."

Related Issue Number 5—Investment Theory versus Investment Practice

The underlying issue here is what decision process should be adopted in efforts to achieve superior performance. On the one hand, most academics support the theory that the price of a stock should equal the risk-adjusted present value of some combination of its future dividends, earnings, and terminal market value. On the other hand, practitioners use a wide variety of techniques, technical and fundamental. In the majority of instances, however, as reflected in the random-walk hypothesis, it does appear most difficult to attain superior performance using conventional decision-making processes. In this regard, J. Lorie and M. Hamilton observe:

Originality, when sound, still has potential for providing rewards. Large financial institutions can seek this originality in techniques of analysis of conventional information, hoping to improve the speed and accuracy with which public information is organized, analyzed, and interpreted. Other security analysts must seek to develop their originality in other ways. Perhaps it will be fruitful to seek new kinds of objective data on corporate performance; perhaps, to view old data in fresh perspectives in order to get a clearer vision of future profitability of individual corporations.[1]

It is the phrase "to view old data in fresh perspectives" that is important in the development of modern security analysis and portfolio management, and critical to this development is the integration of investment theory and investment practice.

We now think in terms of market efficiency, risk versus return, generation of efficient portfolios, capital asset pricing models, and so forth. Indeed, security analysis and portfolio management is broadening to include not only research on the value of specific companies but also on the use of different concepts. For example, utility theory, previously the concern of academics only is now a concern of the practicing financial analyst.

Related Issue Number 6—Understanding Stock Price
Behavior as an Aid in Allocating Economic Resources

Finally, research undertaken to more fully understand the nature of common stock prices is critical to the mechanism by which resources are allocated. As time goes on, this research gains momentum, particularly with the advent of computers and computer-readable data.

A Final Note

This study shows that financial ratios are useful. Practicing investors will reply to this apparently simplistic conclusion that such a statement is obvious, for they have always used financial ratios. In contrast, academics will reply that markets are efficient so that by the time any financial information is known, this information has already been discounted in the price of the stock. Therefore, they argue, financial ratios calculated from historical data generally known to the financial community are not useful. In summary, then, the answers are really not as obvious as one would wish, but the evidence of this study sides with the practitioner.

Notes

Chapter 1
Introduction

1. The term *efficiency of the market place* refers to the speed of the response of stock prices to new information rather than to the stock market operation itself. In this sense, the marketplace is "efficient" if there are no time lags between the time that new information is generally available to the financial community and the time that this information is reflected in the price of an equity. The marketplace is deemed "inefficient" if certain financial ratios or measures generally known to the financial community consistently generate superior risk-adjusted returns. Simply stated, if prices are random, the market place is efficient; if not, the marketplace is inefficient. See William J. Baumol's *The Stock Market and Economic Efficiency* (New York: Fordham University Press, 1965) for a full discussion on the stock market as a mechanism for efficient resource allocation.

2. For example, some recent work of Robert A. Levy and myself on *Analyzing the Analyst (A New Service for Investment Professionals from Hoenig & Strock)*, November 1972, is a first step in this direction.

3. Irwin Friend, Marshal Blume, and Jean Crockett, *Mutual Funds and Other Institutional Investors: A New Perspective* (New York: McGraw-Hill Book Co., 1970).

4. Robert E. Diefenbach, "How Good is Institutional Research?" *Financial Analysts Journal* (September-October 1965); 54-60. Donald M. Peterson, "Stock Market Forecasting—Skill or Chance," (MBA Thesis, Wharton, University of Pennsylvania, 1962).

5. Robert A. Levy, *The Relative Strength Concept of Common Stock Price Forecasting* (Larchmont, N.Y.: Investors Intelligence, 1968).

6. Eugene F. Fama, "Random Walks in Stock Market Prices," *Financial Analysts Journal* 21, no. 5 (September-October 1965): 55-59.

7. J. C. Cragg and Burton Malkiel, "The Consensus and Accuracy of Some Predictions of the Growth of Corporate Earnings," *The Journal of Finance* 23, no. 1 (March 1968).

8. James Lorie et al., *Measuring the Investment Performance of Pension Funds* (Park Ridge, Ill.: Bank Administration Institute, 1968).

9. Walter F. Muhlbach, *Financial Analysis and the Corporate Annual Report* (Washington, D.C.: American University, 1967), 15.

10. Ralph A. Bing, "Survey of Practitioners' Stock Evaluation Methods," *Financial Analysts Journal* 27, no. 3 (May-June 1971).

11. William J. Baumol, *The Stock Market and Economic Efficiency* (New York: Fordham University Press, 1965), 7.

12. VanCourt Hare, Jr., *System Analysis: A Diagnostic Approach* (New York: Harcourt, Brace & World, 1967), pp. 29-30.

13. Benjamin Graham, David L. Dodd, Sidney Cottle, and Charles Tatham, *Security Analysis: Principles and Techniques* (New York: McGraw-Hill Book Co., 1962), p. 486.

Chapter 2
Measuring Risk and Risk-adjusted Returns

1. Harry M. Markowitz, *Portfolio Selection: Efficient Diversification of Investments*. (New York: John Wiley & Sons, 1959).

2. William F. Sharpe, "A Simplified Model for Portfolio Analysis," *Management Science* 9, no. 2 (January 1963), pp. 277-93.

3. Jack L. Treynor, "How to Rate Management of Investment Funds," *Harvard Business Review* 43, no. 1 (January-February 1965), pp. 63-75.

4. Jack L. Treynor and Kay K. Mazuy, "Can Mutual Funds Outguess the Market?" *Harvard Business Review* 44, no. 4 (July-August 1966), p. 131.

5. Robert A. Levy, "On the Short-Term Stationarity of Beta Coefficients," *Financial Analysts Journal* 27, no. 6 (November-December 1971), pp. 55-62.

6. Chris Welles, "The Beta Revolution: Learning to Live with Risk," *Institutional Investor* (September 1971): 21 ff.

7. Michael C. Jensen, "Problems in Selection of Security Portfolios: The Performance of Mutual Funds in the Period 1945-1964." *The Journal of Finance* 23 (May 1968): 389-419.

8. See Fischer Black, Michael C. Jensen, and Myron S. Scholes, "The Capital Asset Pricing Model: Some Empirical Tests," in Michael C. Jensen, ed. *Studies in the Theory of Capital Markets* (New York: Praeger Publishers, 1972).

9. William F. Sharpe, "Mutual Fund Performance," *Journal of Business* 39, pt. 2 (January 1966): 119-138.

10. Treynor, "How to Rate Investment Funds," pp. 63-75.

11. Sharpe, "Mutual Fund Performance," p. 128.

12. Friend, *Mutual Funds*, p. 55.

Chapter 3
Design of the Experiment

1. Robert A. Levy, *The Relative Strength Concept of Common Stock Price Forecasting*. Larchmont, N.Y.: Investors Intelligence, 1968.

2. J.W. Meader, "A Formula for Determining Basic Values Underlying Common Stock Prices," *The Annalist* 46 (November 29, 1935): 749 ff.

3. J.W. Meader, "Stock Price Estimating Formulas, 1930-1939," *The Annalist* 55 (June 27, 1940): 890.

4. For a history of Value Line's methodology; see H. Latane and D. Tuttle, *Security Analysis and Portfolio Managment*, New York: Ronald Press Company (1970), pp. 552-61.

5. Arnold Bernhard, *The Evaluation of Common Stocks*, New York: Simon and Schuster, 1959, p. 95.

6. For example, see J.P. Shelton, "The Value Line Contest: A Test of the Predictability of Stock-Price Changes," *Journal of Business* 40 (July 1967): 251-69.

7. H.A. Latané and W.E. Young, "Test of Portfolio Building Rules," *The Journal of Finance* 24 (September 1969): 595-612.

8. J.L. Evans and S.H. Archer, "Diversification and the Reduction of Dispersion: An Empirical Analysis," *The Journal of Finance* 23 (December 1968): 761-67.

9. Gaumnitz, Jack E. "Investment Diversification under Uncertainty: An Examination of the Number of Securities in a Diversified Portfolio." Unpublished Ph.D dissertation, Stanford University, 1967.

10. Robert A. Levy, "On the Short-Term Stationarity of Beta Coefficients," *Financial Analysts Journal* 27, no. 6 (November-December 1971): 55-62.

Chapter 4
P/E Ratio and Investment Results

1. S. Francis Nicholson, "Price-Earnings Ratios," *Financial Analysts Journal*, 16, no. 4 (July-August 1960): 43-45.

2. Ibid., p. 45.

3. S. Francis Nicholson, "Price Ratios in Relation to Investment

Results,'' *Financial Analysts Journal* 29, no. 1 (January-February 1968): 105-109.

4. James D. McWilliams, "Prices, Earnings and P-E Ratios," *Financial Analysts Journal* 22, no. 3 (May-June 1966): 137-42.

5. Ibid., p. 142.

6. Paul F. Miller and Ernest R. Widman, "Price Performance Outlook for High & Low P/E Stocks," *The Commercial & Financial Chronicle* (September 20, 1966).

7. William Breen, "Low Price-Earnings Ratios and Industry Relatives," *Financial Analysts Journal* 24, no. 4 (July-August 1968): 125-27.

8. Ibid., p. 127.

9. Ibid.

10. Frederick K. Fluegel, "The Rate of Return on High and Low P/E Ratio Stocks," *Financial Analysts Journal* 24, no. 6 (November-December 1968): 130-33.

Chapter 5
Earnings Growth and Investment Results

1. Robert A. Levy and Spero L. Kripotos, "Earnings Growth, P/E's and Relative Strength," *Financial Analysts Journal* 25, no. 6 (November-December 1969): 67.

2. Charles P. Jones and O. Maurice Joy, "Another Look at the Value of P/E Ratios," *Financial Analysts Journal* 26, no. 5 (September-October 1970): 61-64.

3. Niederhoffer, Victor, and Patrick J. Regan, "Earnings Changes, Analysts' Forecasts and Stock Prices," *Financial Analysts Journal* 28, no. 3 (May-June 1972): 65-71.

4. Ibid., p. 71.

5. See, for example, J.G. Cragg and Burton G. Malkiel, "The Consensus and Accuracy of Some Predictions of the Growth of Corporate Earnings," *Journal of Finance* 23, no. 1 (March 1968).

6. Charles P. Jones, "Earnings Trends and Investment Selection," *Financial Analysts Journal* 29 (March-April 1973): 79-83.

Chapter 6
Graham's Valuation Formula and Investment Results

1. Benjamin Graham, David L. Dodd, Sidney Cottle, and Charles

Tatham, *Security Analysis, Principles and Technique* (New York: McGraw-Hill Book Co., 1962), pp. 536-38.

2. Graham, *Security Analysis,* 1962, p. 535.

3. John R. Andrews, "The Fundamental Case for Investing in Growth," *Financial Analysts Journal* Vol 26, no. 6 (November-December, 1970): 55.

Chapter 7
Dividend Yield and Investment Results

1. J.B. Williams, *The Theory of Investment Value*. Cambridge, Mass.: Harvard University Press, 1938.

2. John C. Clendenin and Maurice Van Cleave, "Growth and Common Stock Values," *Journal of Finance* 9 (1954): 365-76.

3. D. Durand, "Growth Stocks and the Petersburg Paradox," *The Journal of Finance* 12, no. 3 (September 1957): 348-63.

4. M.H. Miller and F. Modigliani, "Dividend Policy, Growth and the Valuation of Shares," *Journal of Business* 34 (October 1961): 411-33.

5. M. Gordon, "Optimal Investment and Financing Policy," *The Journal of Finance* 18 (May 1963): 264-72.

6. Graham, *Security Analysis*, p. 517.

7. Ibid., p. 486.

8. Frederick Amling, *Investments: An Introduction to Analysis and Management* (Englewood Cliffs, N.J.: Prentice-Hall, 1970), 15.

9. Douglas Hayes, *Investments: Analysis and Management*, (Toronto, Ont., Macmillan Co., 1969), p. 226.

10. J. Peter Williamson, *Investments: New Analytic Techniques* (New York: Praeger Press, 1971), p. 13.

Chapter 8
Payout Ratio and Investment Results

1. J.B. Williams, *The Theory of Investment Value* (Cambridge, Mass.: Harvard University Press, 1938).

2. For example, see James E. Walter, "Dividend Policy: Its Influence on the Value of the Enterprise," *The Journal of Finance* (May 1963), p. 290.

3. Graham et al., *Security Analysis*, p. 480.

4. Ibid., p. 485.

5. Ibid., p. 485.

6. M.H. Miller and F. Modigliani, "The Cost of Capital, Corporation Finance and the Theory of Investment," *American Economic Review* 48, no. 3 (June 1958). Discussion of the Modigliani-Miller thesis is found in Chapter 7.

7. M. Nerlove, "Factors Affecting Differences Among Rates of Return on Investments in Individual Common Stocks," *Review of Economics and Statistics* 1, no. 3 (August 1968): 312-31.

8. Ibid., p. 319.

9. Irwin Friend and Marshall Puckett, "Dividends and Stock Prices," *American Economic Review* 54 (September 1964): 656-82.

10. Ibid., p. 682.

Chapter 9
Dividend Changes and Investment Results

1. Myron J. Gordon, "Dividends, Earnings, and Stock Prices," *The Review of Economics and Statistics,* 41, no. 2 (May 1959): 99-105.

2. Ibid., p. 101.

3. Ibid., p. 104.

4. Ibid., p. 105.

Chapter 10
Total Invested Capital and Investment Results

1. Ian M. D. Little, "Higgledy Piggledy Growth," *Institute of Statistics* 24, no. 4 (Oxford: November 1962): 387-412.

2. R. Minturn Sedgwick, "The Record of Conventional Investment Management," *Financial Analysts Journal* 29, no. 4 (July-August 1973): 41-44.

3. Ibid., p. 41.

4. Ibid., p. 41.

5. Ibid., p. 44.

Chapter 11
Rate of Return on Invested Capital and Investment Results

1. Robert P. Colin, *Summary Economic/Market Review and Outlook,* Faulkner, Dawkins & Sullivan, May 31, 1972.

Chapter 12
Debt/Capital Ratio and Investment Results

1. See, for example, Franco Modigliani and Merton Miller, "The Cost of Capital, Corporate Finance, and the Theory of Investment," *American Economic Review* (June 1958): 261-97.

2. Modigliani and Miller, "Cost of Capital," pp. 261-97, and "Corporate Income Taxes and the Cost of Capital: A Correction," *American Economic Review* 53, no. 3 (1963): 433-43.

3. Ibid., p. 278.

4. H. Benishay, "Variability in Earnings-Price Ratios of Corporate Equities," *American Economic Review* (March 1961): 81-94.

5. Ibid., p. 86.

6. Ibid., p. 93.

7. William P. O'Connor, Jr., *The 14 Point Method for Beating the Market* (Chicago, Ill.: Henry Regnery Company, 1972).

8. Ibid., p. 35.

Chapter 14
The Principle of Strategy before Selection

1. Graham et al., *Security Analysis, Principles and Technique* (New York: McGraw-Hill Book Co., 1962), p. 530.

Chapter 15
Conclusions

1. J.H. Lorie and M.T. Hamilton, *The Stock Market: Theories and Evidence* (Homewood, Ill.: Richard D. Irwin, 1973), p. 109.

Bibliography

Books

Amling, Frederick. *Investments*: *An Introduction to Analysis and Management*. Englewood Cliffs, N.J.: Prentice-Hall, 1970.

Baumol, William J. *The Stock Market and Economic Efficiency*. New York: Fordham University Press, 1965.

Bernhard, A. *The Evaluation of Common Stocks*. New York: Simon and Schuster, 1959.

Brealey, Richard A. *An Introduction to Risk and Return from Common Stocks*. Cambridge, Mass.: M.I.T. Press, 1969.

Clarkson, Geoffrey P. E. *Portfolio Selection*: *A Simulation of Trust Investment*. Englewood Cliffs, N.J.: Prentice-Hall, 1962.

Cohen, Jerome B. and Edward D. Zinbarg. *Investment Analysis and Portfolio Management*. Homewood, Ill.: Richard D. Irwin, 1967. Chapter 20, "The Role of the Computer," 732-67.

Cohen, Kalman J. and Frederick S. Hammer, eds. *Analytic Methods in Banking*. Homewood, Ill.: Richard D. Irwin, 1966. Part IV, "Trust Departments," 255-378.

Cootner, Paul H., ed. *The Random Character of Stock Market Prices*. Cambridge, Mass.: M.I.T. Press, 1964.

Edwards, Robert D. and John Magee. *Technical Analysis of Stock Trends*. Springfield, Mass.: John Magee, 1964.

Encyclopedia of Stock Market Techniques. Larchmont, N.Y.: Investors Intelligence, 1970.

Farrar, Donald. *The Investment Decision Under Uncertainty*. Englewood Cliffs, N.J.: Prentice-Hall, 1962.

Frederickson, E. Bruce, ed. *Frontiers of Investment Analysis*. Scranton, Pa.: International Textbook Co., 1966.

Friend, Irwin, Marshall Blume, and Jean Crockett. *Mutual Funds and Other Institutional Investors: A New Perspective*. New York: McGraw-Hill Book Co., 1970.

Graham, Benjamin. *The Intelligent Investor*. New York: Harper & Row, 1973.

Graham, Benjamin, David L. Dodd, Sidney Cottle, and Charles Tatham. *Security Analysis, Principles and Technique*. New York: McGraw-Hill Book Co., 1962.

Hayes, Douglas A. *Investments: Analysis and Management*. New York: Macmillan Co., 1966.

Jensen, Michael C., ed. *Studies in the Theory of Capital Markets*. New York: Praeger Publishers, 1972.

Latane, H. and D. Tuttle. *Security Analysis and Portfolio Management*, New York: Ronald Press Company, 1970.

Lerner, Eugene and Willard T. Carlston. *A Theory of Financial Analysis*. New York: Harcourt, Brace and World, 1966.

Levy, Robert A. *The Relative Strength Concept of Common Stock Price Forecasting*. Larchmont, N.Y.: Investors Intelligence, 1968.

Lorie, James H. et al. *Measuring the Investment Performance of Pension Funds*. Park Ridge, Ill.: Bank Administration Institute, 1968; and M. T. Hamilton, *The Stock Market: Theories and Evidence*. Homewood, Ill.: Richard P. Irwin, 1973.

Markowitz, Harry M. *Portfolio Selection: Efficient Diversification of Investment*. New York: John Wiley & Sons, 1959.

Moore, Basil J. *An Introduction to the Theory of Finance*. New York: Free Press, 1968.

O'Connor, William P. *The 14 Point Method for Beating the Market*, Chicago: Henry Regnery Co., 1971.

VanCourt, Hare, Jr. *System Analysis: A Diagnostic Approach*. New York: Harcourt, Brace & World, 1967.

Williams, J.B. *The Theory of Investment Value*. Cambridge, Mass.: Harvard University Press, 1938.

Williamson, J. Peter. *Investments: New Analytic Techniques*. New York: Praeger Press, 1971.

Wee, Hsiu-Kwang, and Alan J. Zakon, eds. *Elements of Investments*. New York: Holt, Rinehart and Winston, 1965.

Zarnowitz, Victor. *An Appraisal of Short-Term Economic Forecasts*. New York: National Bureau of Economic Research, 1967.

Periodicals

Alexander, Sidney S. "Price Movements in Speculative Markets: Trends or Random Walks," *Industrial Management Review* 2 (May 1961): 7-26.

Andrews, John R. "The Fundamental Case for Investing in Growth," *Financial Analysts Journal* 26, no. 6 (November-December 1970): 55-64.

Aranyi, Janos. "Portfolio Diversification," *Financial Analysts Journal* 23, no. 5 (September-October 1967).

Arditti, Fred D. "Risk and the Required Return on Equity," *Journal of Finance* 22 (March 1967): 19-36.

Babcock, Guilford C. "The Concept of Sustainable Growth," *Financial Analysts Journal* 26, no. 3 (May-June 1970): 108-114.

Bauman, W. Scott. "Evaluation of Prospective Investment Performance," *Financial Analysts Journal* 24, no. 3 (May-June 1968): 276-95.

———. "Investment Analysis: Science or Fiction?" *Financial Analysts Journal* 23, no. 1 (January-February 1967): 93-97.

———, and Thomas A Klein. "Investment Profit Correlation," *Michigan Business Reports* 55 (July 1967): 1-51.

Baumol, William J. "An Expected Gain-Confidence Limit Criterion for Portfolio Selection," *Management Science* 10, no. 1 (October 1963): 174-82.

———. "On Dividend Policy and Market Imperfection," *The Journal of Business* (January 1963): 112-15.

———. "Mathematical Analysis of Portfolio Selection," *Financial Analysts Journal* 22 no. 5 (September-October 1966): 95-99.

Bean, Alan M. "Portfolio Analysis and Stock Selection by Computer," *Financial Executive* (February 1967): 26-36.

Bell, Edward W. "The Price-Future Earnings Ratios: A Practical Aid to Stock Valuation," *Analysts Journal* 14 (August 1958): 25-28.

Benishay, Haskel. "Variability in Earnings-Price Ratios of Corporate Equities,: *American Economic Review* (March 1961): 81-94.

Bing, Ralph A. "Scientific Investment Analysis, A Comment," *Financial Analysts Journal* 23, no. 3 (May-June 1967): 97-98.

———. "Survey of Practitioners Stock Evaluation Methods," *Financial Analysts Journal* 27, no. 3 (May-June 1971).

Block, Frank E. "Risk and Performance," *Financial Analysts Journal* 22, no. 2 (March-April 1966): 65-74.

———. "Elements of Portfolio Construction," *Financial Analysts Journal* 25, no. 3 (May-June 1969).

Blume, Marshall E. "Portfolio Theory: A Step Toward Its Practical Application," *The Journal of Business* (April 1970): 152-73.

Bolster, Richard L. "The Relationship of Monetary Policy to the Stock Market: The Experience with Margin Requirements," *The Journal of Finance* (September 1967).

Bower, Richard S. and Ronald F. Wippern. "Risk-Return Measurement in Portfolio Selection and Performance Appraisal Models: Progress Report," *Journal of Financial and Quantitative Analysis* 4, no. 4 (December 1969): 417-47.

Brada, J.C., H. Ernst and J. Van Tassel. "The Distribution of Stock Price Differences: Gaussian After All?" *Operations Research* (April 1966).

Breen, William. "Low Price-Earnings Ratios and Industry Relatives," *Financial Analysts Journal* 24, no. 4 (July-August 1968): 125-27.

————, and James Savage, "Portfolio Distribution and Tests of Security Selection Models," *Journal of Finance* 23, no. 5 (December 1968): 805-19.

Bringham, Eugene and James Pappas. "Rates of Return on Common Stocks," *The Journal of Business* (July 1969): 302-316.

————."Duration of Growth, Changes in Growth Rates and Corporate Share Prices," *Financial Analysts Journal* 22, no. 3 (May-June 1966): 157-62.

Buff, Jerome H., Gorden Biggar, and Gary Burkhead. "The Application of New Decision Analysis Techniques to Investment Research," *Financial Analysts Journal* 24 no. 6 (November-December 1968): 123-28.

Chottiner, Sherman. "Optimal Investor-Stock Market Efficiency Standard," *Financial Analysts Journal* 20, no. 1 (January-February).

————, Nicholis Moldovsky, and Catherine May. "Common Stock Valuation-Principles, Tables and Application," *Financial Analysts Journal* 21, no. 2 (March-April).

Clarkson, Geoffrey, and Allen Meltzer. "Portfolio Selection: A Heuristic Approach," *Journal of Finance* (December 1960): 465-80.

Clendenin, John, and M. Van Cleave. "Growth and Common Stock Values," *Journal of Finance* 9 (September 1954): 365-76.

Cohen, Kalman, and Edwin Elton. "Inter-Temporal Portfolio Analysis Based on Simulation of Joint Returns," *Management Science* 14, no. 1 (September 1967): 5-18.

————, and Jerry Pogue. "An Empirical Evaluation of Alternative Portfolio Selection Models," *Journal of Business* 40 (April 1967): 166-93.

Colin, Robert P. "Summary Economic/Market Review and Outlook," Faulkner, Dawkins & Sullivan, May 31, 1972.

————, and Jerry Pogue. "Some Comments Concerning Mutual Fund versus Random Portfolio Performance," *Journal of Business* 41 (April 1968): 180-90.

Cootner, Paul H. "Stock Prices: Random vs. Systematic Changes," *Industrial Management Review* 3, no. 2 (Spring 1962): 24-45.

Courtney, Thomas. "Research Today—Or, Who's Afraid of Random Walk?" *Investors Securities* (September 1970): 21-25, 33.

Cowles, A. "A Revision of Previous Conclusions Regarding Stock Price Behavior," *Econometrica* (October 1960): 909-915.

————. "Can Stock Market Forecasters Forecast.?" *Econometrica* 1, no. 3 (1933): 315.

Cragg, Jr. G. and Burton Malkiel. "The Consensus and Accuracy of Some Predictions of the Growth of Corporate Earnings," *Journal of Finance* 23, no. 1 (March 1968): 67-84.

Diefenbach, Robert E. "How Good is Institutional Research?" *Financial Analysts Journal* 21, no. 5 (September-October 1965).

Dietz, Peter. "Measurement of Performance of Security Portfolios-Components of a Measurement Model: Rate of Return, Risk and Timing," *Journal of Finance* (May 1968): 267-75.

Durand, David. "Growth Stocks and the Petersburg Paradox," *Journal of Finance* 12, no. 3 (September 1957): 348-63.

Edwards, Charles, and James Hilton. "A Note on the High-Low Price Average as an Estimator of Annual Average Stock Prices," *Journal of Finance* (March 1966): 112-15.

Elliot, David. "A New Index of Equity Values," *Financial Analysts Journal* 25, no. 3 (May-June 1969).

Evans, John L. "The Random-Walk Hypothesis, Portfolio Analysis and the Buy-And-Hold Criterion," *Journal of Financial and Quantitative Analysis* 3, no. 3 (September 1968): 327-41.

————, and S. H. Archer. "Diversification and the Reduction of Dispersion: An Empirical Analysis," *The Journal of Finance* 23 (December 1968): 761-67.

Fama, Eugene F. "Mandelbrot and the Stable Paretian Hypothesis," *Journal of Business* 36 (October 1963): 420-29.

————. "Portfolio Analysis in a Stable Paretian Market," *Management Science* 11 (January 1965): 404-419.

————. "The Behavior of Stock-Market Prices," *Journal of Business* 37, no. 1 (January 1965): 34-105.

————. "Tomorrow on the New York Stock Exchange," *Journal of Business* (July 1965): 285-99.

————. Random Walks in Stock-Market Prices," *Financial Analysts Journal* 21, no. 5 (September-October 1965): 55-59.

————, and Marshall E. Blume, "Filter Rules and Stock-Market Trading," *Journal of Business* 39 (January 1966): 226-41.

————. "Risk, Return and Equilibrium: Some Clarifying Comments," *Journal of Finance* (March 1968): 29-40.

————. et al. "The Adjustment of Stock Prices to New Information," *International Economic Review* 10 (February 1969): 1-26.

Ferber, R. "Short-Run Effects of Stock Market Services on Stock Prices," *Journal of Finance* 13 (March 1958): 80-95.

Feuerstein, Alan E., and Peter G. Maggi. "Computer Investment Research," *Financial Analysts Journal* 24, no. 1 (January-February 1968).

_____. "Computer Portfolio Analysis," *Mid-Western Banker* (March 1967).

_____. "Computer Applications to Investment Research," *Investments Dealers Digest* (July 10, 1967).

_____, and Manown Kisor. "Towards a Valuation Model Employing Historical Constructs as Proxies for Analysts Expectations," *Presentation at the Seminar on the Analysis of Security Prices*, University of Chicago (May 1, 1967).

Fischer, G.R. "Some Factors Influencing Share Prices," *Economic Journal* 71, no. 281 (March 1961): 121-41.

Fischer, Lawrence. "Outcomes for Random Investments in Common Stocks Listed on the New York Stock Exchange," *Journal of Business* 38, no. 2 (April 1965): 149-61.

_____. "Some New Stock-Market Indexes," *Journal of Business*, 39 (January 1966): 191-225.

_____, and J.H. Lorie. "Rates of Return on Investments in Common Stocks," *Journal of Business* 37, no. 1 (January 1, 1969): 1-21.

_____, and J.H. Lorie. "Some Studies of Variability of Returns on Investments in Common Stocks," *Journal of Business* (April 1970).

_____, and J.H. Lorie, "Rates of Return on Investments in Common Stock: The Year-By-Year Record, 1926-65," *Journal of Business* 41, no. 3 (July 1968): 291-316.

Fiske, Heide. "The Computer: How It is Changing the Money Managers," *The Institutional Investor* (April 1968): 23-81.

Fitch, Bruce and Kalman Cohen. "The Average Investment Performance Index," *Management Science* (February 1966).

Fluegel, Frederick. "The Rate of Return on High and Low P/E Ratio Stocks," *Financial Analysts Journal* 24, no. 6 (November-December 1968): 130-33.

Foster, Earl M. *The Price Earnings Ratio and Growth, Financial Analysts Journal* 26, no. 1 (January-February 1970): 96-99.

_____. "Growth and P/E Ratio: A Revision. *Financial Analysts Journal* 26, no. 4 (July-August 1970): 115-18.

Friend, Irwin, and Douglas Vickers. "Portfolio Selection and Investment Performance," *Journal of Finance* 20, no. 3 (September 1965): 391-415.

_____. "Re-Evaluation of Alternative Portfolio-Selection Models," *Journal of Business* (April 1968): 174-79.

Friend, Irwin, and Marshall Puckett. "Dividends and Stock Prices," *American Economic Review* 54 (September 1964): 650-82.

Gal, Joseph. "Man-Machine Interactive Systems and their Application to

Financial Analysis," *Financial Analysts Journal* 22, no. 3 (May-June 1966).

Gruber, Martin. "Determinants of Common Stock Prices," *The Journal of Finance* (December 1966).

Gaubis, Anthony. "The Timing Factors in Business and Stock Market Forecasting," *Financial Analysts Journal* 29, no. 2 (March-April 1963): 19-23.

Godrey, Michael, C.W.J. Granger, and O. Morgenstern. "The Random Walk Hypothesis of Stock Market Behavior," *Kyklos* 17 (January 1964): 1-30.

Gorden, Myron. "Security and Investment: Theory and Evidence," *Journal of Finance* 19, no. 4 (December 1964): 607-618.

————. "Dividends, Earnings and Stock Prices," *The Review of Economics and Statistics* 41, no. 2 (May 1969): 99-105.

————. "Optimal Investment and Financing Policy," *The Journal of Finance* 18 (May 1963): 264-72.

Gould, Alex, and Maurice Buchsbaum. "A Filter Approach to Stock Selection," *Financial Analysts Journal* 25, no. 6 (November-December 1969): 61 ff.

Graber, Dean. "Real and Illusory Earnings Growth," *Financial Analysts Journal* 25, no. 2 (March-April 1969).

Granger, C.W.J. "Some Aspects of the Random Walk Model of Stock Market Prices," *International Economic Review* 9, no. 2 (June 1968).

————, and O. Morgenstern. "Spectral Analysis of New York Stock Exchange Prices," *Kyklos* 16 (January 1963): 1-27.

————. "What the Random Walk Model Does Not Say," *Financial Analysts Journal* 26, no. 3 (May-June 1970): 91-93.

Gray, William. "Measuring the Analysts Performance," *Financial Analysts Journal* 22, no. 3 (March-April 1966).

Green, David, and Joel Segall. "The Predictive Power of First-Quarter Earnings Reports," *Journal of Business* (January 1967): 44-55.

Green, Paul E., and Arun Maheshwar. "Common Stock Perception and Preference: An Amplication of Multidimensional Scaling," *Journal of Business* (July 1969).

Groome, James J. "Breakthrough Ahead in Management Information," *Burrough's Clearing House* (March 1967).

Gumperz, Julian. "Machines that Analyze-or Analysts?" *Financial Analysts Journal* 23, no. 1 (January-February 1966): 93.

Hall, Parker J. "Toward Effective Portfolio Management," *Financial Analysts Journal* 22, no. 1 (January-February 1966): 93.

Hanoch, G., and H. Levy. "Efficient Portfolio Selection with Quadratic and Cubic Utility," *Journal of Business* (April 1970).

Harkavy, Oscar. "The Relation between Retained Earnings and Common Stock Prices for Large Listed Corporations," *Journal of Finance* 8 (September 1953): 283-97.

Hartwell, John M. "Performance, Its Promise and Problems," *Financial Analysts Journal* 25, no. 2 (March-April 1969).

Hastie, Larry D. "The Determination of Optimal Investment Policy," *Management Science* 13, no. 12 (August 1967): 757-74.

Hausman, Warren H. "A Note on the Value Line Contest: A Test on the Predictability of Stock-Price Changes," *Journal of Business* (July 1969): 317-20.

Hayes, Douglas A. "The Undervalued Issue Strategy," *Financial Analysts Journal* 23, no. 3 (May-June 1967): 121-27.

Heins, James, and Stephen Allison. "Some Factors Affecting Stock Price Variability," *Journal of Business* (January 1966): 19-23.

Herzog, John P. "Investor Experience in Corporate Securities: A New Technique for Measurement," *Journal of Finance* 19 (March 1964): 46-62.

Hirshleifer, Jack. "Investment Decision under Uncertainty: Application of the State-Preference Approach," *The Quarterly Journal of Economics* 80 (May 1966): 252-77.

————. "On the Theory of Optimal Investment," *Journal of Political Economy* 64, no. 4 (August 1958): 329-52.

Hoffland, David L. "The Folklore of Wall Street," *Financial Analysts Journal* (May-June 1967): 85-88.

Holt, C. C. "The Influence of Growth Duration on Share Prices," *Journal of Finance* 17 (September 1962): 465-75.

Horowitz, Ira. "The Reward to Variability Ratio and Mutual Fund Performance," *Journal of Business* 39 (October 1966): 485-88.

————. "A Model for Mutual Fund Evaluation," *Industrial Management Review* 6 (Spring 1965): 81-92.

Houthakker, Hendrick. "Systematic and Random Elements in Short-term Price Movements," *American Economic Review Papers and Proceedings* 51, no. 2 (May 1961): 164-72.

————. "How to Buy Stocks by the Calendar," *Fortune* 71 (March 1965): 62.

James, F.E. "Monthly Moving Averages—An Effective Investment Tool?," *Journal of Financial and Quantitative Analysis* 3, no. 3 (September 1968): 315-26.

Jensen, Michael C. "Random Walks: Reality or Myth-Comment," *Financial Analysts Journal* 23 no. 6 (November-December 1967): 77-85.

_____. Problems in Selection of Security Portfolios: The Performance of Mutual Funds in the Period 1945-1964," *Journal of Finance* 23 (May 1968): 389-411.

_____. "Risk, The Pricing of Capital Assets, and the Evaluation of Investment Portfolios," *Journal of Business* 42 (April 1969): 167-248.

Jones, Charles H. "The Growth Rate Appraiser," *Financial Analysts Journal* 24, no. 5 (September-October 1968): 109-111.

_____. "Earnings Trends and Investment Selection," *Financial Analysts Journal* 29 (March-April 1973): 79-83.

Jones, C.P. and R.H. Litzenberger. "Earnings Seasonality and Stock Prices," *Financial Analysts Journal* 25, no. 6 (November-December 1969): 57-59.

_____, and M. Joy. "Productive Value of P/E Ratios," *Financial Analysts Journal* 26, no. 5 (September-October 1970): 61-64.

_____, and M. Joy. "Another Look at the Value of P/E Ratios," *Financial Analysts Journal* 26, no. 5 (September-October 1970): 61-64.

Kahl, Alfred L. "Computers and Investment Management," *Georgia Business* (June 1968).

Kaufman, Gorden M. "Sequential Investment Analysis Under Uncertainty," *Journal of Business* (January 1963).

Kendall, M.G. "The Analysis of Economic Time-Series—Part I: Prices," *Journal of the Royal Statistical Society* 26, pt. I (1953): 11-25.

King, Benjamin F. "Market and Industry Factors in Stock Price Behavior," *Journal of Business* 39, pt. II (January 1966) 139-90.

Kisor, Manown. "Quantitative Approaches to Common Stock Selection," *Business Economics* (Spring 1966): 16-23.

_____. "The Financial Aspects of Growth," *Financial Analysts Journal* 20, no. 2 (March-April 1964),

_____, and Van A. Messner. "The Filter Approach and Earnings Forecasts," *Financial Analysts Journal* 25, no. 1 (January-February 1969): 109-115.

Kotler, Philip. "Elements in a Theory of Growth Stock Valuation," *Financial Analysts Journal* 18, no. 3 (May-June 1962): 35-46.

Lamberton, D. Mel. "Economic Growth and Stock Prices, The Australian Experience," *Journal of Business* (July 1958): 200-210.

Latane, Henry, and Donald L. Tuttle. "Framework for Forming Probability Beliefs," *Financial Analysts Journal* 24, no. 4 (July-August 1968): 51-61.

————, and Donald L. Tuttle. "Criteria for Portfolio Building," *Journal of Finance* 22, no. 3 (September 1967): 359-73.

————, and Donald L. Tuttle. "P/E Ratios V. Changes in Earnings in Forecasting Future Price Changes," *Financial Analysts Journal* 25, no. 1 (January-February 1969): 117-20.

————. "Investment Criteria—A Three Asset Portfolio Balance Model," *The Review of Economics and Statistics* 45 (November 1963): 427-30.

————, and W. E. Young. "Tests of Portfolio Building Rules," *The Journal of Finance*, 24 (September 1969), 595-612.

Lerner, Eugene, and Rolf Auster. "Does the Market Discount Potential Dilution?" *Financial Analysts Journal* 25, no. 4 (July-August 1969).

————, and W. T. Couleton. "A Model for the Determination of Security Prices," *Business Economics* (Spring 1966): 24-27.

Levy, Robert A. "Random Walks: Reality or Myth," *Financial Analysts Journal* 23, no. 6 (November-December 1967): 69-77.

————. "The Principle of Portfolio Upgrading," *Industrial Management Review* (Fall 1967): 82-96.

————. "The Theory of Random Walks: A Survey of Findings," *The American Economist* 11 (Fall 1967): 34-38.

————. "Measurement of Investment Performance," *Journal of Financial and Quantitative Analysis* 3 (March 1968): 35-38.

————, and Spero L. Kripotos. "An Empirical Investigation of Chart Consolidation Patterns," *Securities*, no. 10 (October-November 1970): 21 ff.

————, and Spero L. Kripotos. "Earnings Growth, P/E's and Relative Price Strength," *Financial Analysts Journal* 25, no. 6 (November-December 1969).

————. "On the Short-Term Stationarity of Beta Coefficients," *Financial Analysts Journal* 27, no. 6 (November-December 1971): 55-62.

Lintner, John. "Security Prices, Risk and Maximal Gains from Diversification," *Journal of Finance* 20, no. 4 (December 1965): 587-615.

————. "The Aggregation of Investor's Diverse Judgements and Preferences in Purely Competitive Security Markets," *Journal of Finance and Quantitative Analysis* 4, no. 4 (December 1969): 347-400.

————. "The Market Price of Risk, Size of Market and Investor's Risk Aversion," *Review of Economics and Statistics* (February 1970).

Little, I.M.D. "Higgledy Piggledy Growth," Oxford Institute of Statistics Bulletin, Oxford, England (November 1962): 387-412.

Lorie, James H., and Lawrence Fisher. "Knowledge Makes A Difference," *Financial Analysts Journal* 21, no. 6 (November-December 1965): 118-120.

————. "Preliminary Comments: NABAC Study on Measuring Investment Performance of Pension Funds," *Financial Analysts Journal* 24, no. 2 (March-April 1968): 139-43.

Lyons, John F. "What Makes a Performance Manager Sell Your Stocks?," *Investment Banking and Corporate Financing* (Winter 1968).

Machol, Robert E., and Eugene M. Lerner. "Risk, Ruin and Investment Analysis," *Journal of Financial and Quantitative Analysis* 4, no. 4 (December 1969): 473-92.

Malkiel, Burton G. "Equity Yields, Growth and the Structure of Share Prices," *American Economic Review* (December 1963): 1004-31.

Mandelbrot, Benoit. "The Variation of Speculative Prices," *Journal of Business* 36 (October 1963): 394-419.

————. "The Variation of Some Other Speculative Prices," *Journal of Business* (October 1967): 393-413.

————. "Forecasts of Future Prices, Unbiased Markets, and 'Martingale' Models," *Journal of Business* 39 (January 1966): 242-55.

Mao, James C.T. "The Valuation of Growth Stocks: The Investment Opportunities Approach," *The Journal of Finance* (March 1966): 95-102.

————, and Carl E. Sarndal. "A Decision Theory Approach to Portfolio Selection," *Management Science* 12, no. 8 (April 1966): 323-33.

Martin, A.D. "Mathematical Programming of Portfolio Selections," *Management Science* 1 (January 1955): 152-66.

Masica, Joseph S. "Corporate Earnings Predictions," *Financial Analysts Journal* 25, no. 4 (July-August 1969): 107-110.

Mayor, Thomas H. "Short Trading Activities and the Price of Equities: Some Simulation and Repression Results," *Journal of Financial and Quantitative Analysis*, 3, no. 3 (September 1968): 283-98.

McCandlish, Randolf. "Some Methods for Measuring Performance of a Pension Fund," *Financial Analysts Journal* 21, no. 6 (November-December 1965).

McKenzie, Robert R. "A Computer Simulation Used to Evaluate Alternative Financial Strategies," *The Journal of Finance* (September 1965).

McQuown, John A. "The Application of Computers & Investment Decision Making," *Investment Dealers Digest* (July 10, 1967).

McWilliams, James D. "Prices, Earnings and P/E Ratios," *Financial Analysts Journal* 22, no. 3 (May-June 1966): 137-42.

Meader, J.W. "A Formula for Determining Basic Values Underlying Common Stock Prices," *The Annalist* 46 (November 29, 1935): 749 ff.

————. "Stock Price Estimating Formulas, 1930-1939," *The Annalist* 55 (June 27, 1940): 890.

Meyerholz, John C. "Competition and Investment Management," *Financial Analysts Journal* 22, no. 1 (January-February 1966): 97-105.

Miller, M., and Franco Modigliani. "Dividend Policy, Growth and the Valuation of Shares," *Journal of Business*, 34 (October 1961): 411-33.

Miller, Paul, and Ernest Widman. "Price Performance Outlook for High and Low P/E Stocks," *The Commerical and Financial Chronicle* (September 20, 1966).

————. "The Cost of Capital, Corporation Finance and the Theory of Investment," *American Economic Review* 48, no. 3 (June 1958).

Molodovsky, Nicholas. "Some Aspects of Price Earnings Ratios," *The Analysts Journal* (May 1953): 65-78.

————. "Stock Values and Stock Prices," *Financial Analysts Journal* 24, no. 6 (November-December, 1968): 134-48.

————. "A Theory of Price Earnings Ratios," *The Analysts Journal* (November 1953): 65-80.

————. "Selecting Growth Stocks," *Financial Analysts Journal* 24, no. 5 (September-October 1968): 103-106.

————. "Stock Market: Lessons from the Recent Past," *Financial Analysts Journal* 20, no. 1 (January-February 1964): 50-51.

————. "Recent Studies of P/E Ratios," *Financial Analysts Journal* 23, no. 3 (May-June 1967): 101-110.

————. "Building a Stock Market Measure—A Case Story," *Financial Analysts Journal* 23, no. 3 (May-June 1967): 43-46.

————. "Valuation of Common Stocks," *Financial Analysts Journal* 15 (January-February 1959): 23-27, 84-99.

Mossin, Jan. "Optimal Multiperiod Portfolio Policies," *Journal of Business* (April 1968): 215-29.

Murphy, Joseph E. "Returns on Equity Capital, Dividend Payout and Growth of Earnings Per Share," *Financial Analysts Journal* 24, no. 3 (May-June 1967): 91-93.

————, and Harold W. Stevenson. "Price/Earnings Ratios and Future Growth of Earnings and Dividends," *Financial Analysts Journal* 23, no. 6 (November-December 1967): 113.

————, and Russell J. Nelson. "A Note on the Stability of P/E Ratios," *Financial Analysts Journal* 25, no. 2 (March-April 1969).

————. "Relative Growth in Earnings Per Share-Past and Future," *Financial Analysts Journal* 21, no. 6 (November-December 1966): 73-76.

————. "Earnings Growth and Price Changes in the Same Time Period," *Financial Analysts Journal* 23, no. 1 (January-February 1968): 97-99.

National Bureau of Economic Research. "Research in the Capital Markets," *Journal of Finance* 19 (Supplement: May 1964): 1-43.

Nerlove, M. "Factors Affecting Differences among Rates of Return on Investments in Individual Common Stocks," *Review of Economics and Statistics* 1, no. 3 (August 1968).

Nicholas, Donald A. "A Note on Inflation and Common Stock Values," *Journal of Finance* 23, no. 4 (September 1968): 655-57.

Nicholson, Francis S. "Price Ratios in Relation to Investment Results," *Financial Analysts Journal* 24, no. 1 (January-February 1968): 105-109.

_____. "Price Earnings Ratios," *Financial Analysts Journal* 16, no. 4 (July-August 1960): 43-45.

Niederhoffer, Victor. "Clustering of Stock Prices," *Operations Research* 13 (March 1965): 258-65.

_____. "A New Look at Clustering of Stock Prices," *Journal of Business* (April 1966).

_____, and M.F.M. Osborne. "Market Making and Reversal on the Stock Exchange," *Journal of the American Statistical Association* 61 (December 1966): 897-916.

_____, and Patrick J. Regan. "Earnings Changes, Analysts Forecasts and Stock Prices," *Financial Analysts Journal* 28, no. 3 (May-June 1972): 65-71.

Osborne, M.F.M. "Brownian Motion in the Stock Market," *Operations Research* 7, no. 2 (March-April 1959): 145-73.

_____. "Periodic Structure in the Brownian Motion of Stock Prices," *Operations Research* 10, no. 3 (May-June 1962): 345-79.

_____. "Some Quantitative Tests for Stock Price Generating Models and Trading Folklore." *Journal of the American Statistical Association* 62 (June 1967): 321-40.

Owen, Joel. "Analysis of Variance Tests for Local Trends in the Standard and Poor's Index," *Journal of Finance* (June 1968): 509-514.

Pratt, John W. "Risk Aversion in the Small and in the Large," *Econometrica* 32 (January-April 1964): 122-36.

Press, James S. "A Compound Events Model for Security Prices," *Journal of Business* (July 1967): 317-35.

Pye, Gorden. "Portfolio Selection and Security Prices," *Review of Economics and Statistics* (February 1967).

Reints, William W. "Investment Criteria of Open-End Investment Companies: An Empirical Investigation," *Journal of Finance* (September 1967).

Renshaw, Edward F. "The Random Walk Hypothesis, Performance

Measurement and Portfolio Theory," *Financial Analysts Journal* 24, no. 2 (March-April, 1968).

―――――. "Estimating the Return on S&P's Industrial Price Index," *Financial Analysts Journal* 25, no. 1 (January-February 1969): 121-23.

―――――. "Portfolio Balance Models in Perspective: Some Generalizations That Can Be Derived from the Two-Asset Case," *Journal of Financial and Quantitative Analysis* 2, no. 2 (June 1967): 123-49.

―――――, and Renshaw, V.D. "Test of the Random Walk Hypothesis," *Financial Analysts Journal* 26, no. 5 (September-October 1970): 51-59.

Renwick, Fred B. "Theory of Investment Behavior and Empirical Analysis of Stock Market Price Relatives," *Management Science* 15, no. 1 (September 1968): 57-71.

―――――. "Asset Management and Investor Portfolio Behavior: Theory and Practice," *Journal of Finance* 24, no. 2 (May 1969): 181-206.

Richardson, Lemont K. "Do High Risks Lead to High Returns?" *Financial Analysts Journal* 26, no. 2 (March-April 1970): 88-99.

Roberts, Harry V. "Stock-Market 'Patterns' and Financial Analysis: Methodological Suggestions," *Journal of Finance* 14, no. 1 (March 1959): 1-10.

Robichek, Alexander A. "Risk and the Value of Securities," *Journal of Financial and Quantitative Analysis*, IV, No. 4 (December, 1969), 513-538.

―――――, and S. Myers. "Valuation of the Firm: Effects of Uncertainty in a Market Context," *Journal of Finance* 21, no. 2 (May 1966): 215-28.

Samuelson, Paul A. "Proof that Properly Anticipated Prices Fluctuate Randomly," *Industrial Management Review* 6 (Spring 1965): 41-50.

―――――. ."Efficient Portfolio Selection for Pareto-Levy Investments," *Journal of Financial and Quantitative Analysis* 2, no. 2 (June 1967): 107-122.

―――――. "General Proof that Diversification Pays," *The Journal of Financial and Quantitative Analysis* (March 1967): 1-13.

Sarnot, Marshall, and Haim Ban-Shahar. "Reinvestment and the Rate of Return in Common Stocks," *Journal of Finance* 21 (December 1966).

Savage, James, and William Breen. "Portfolio Distribution and Tests of Security Models," *Journal of Finance*.

Schneider, Theodore H. "A Worksheet Technique for Measuring Performance," *Financial Analysts Journal* 25, no. 3 (May-June 1969).

Sedgwick, R. Minturn. "The Record of Conventional Investment Management," *Financial Analysts Journal* 29, no. 4 (July-August 1973): 41-44.

Seelenfreund, Alan, George G. C. Parker, and James C. Van Horne.

"Stock Price Behavior and Trading," *Journal of Financial and Quantitative Analysis* 3, no. 3 (September 1968): 263-81.

Sharpe, William F. "Capital Asset Prices: A Theory of Market Equilibrium under Conditions of Risk," *Journal of Finance* 19, no. 3 (September 1964): 425-42.

_____. "Risk-Aversion in the Stock Market: Some Empirical Evidence," *Journal of Finance* 20, no. 4 (September 1965): 416-22.

_____. "Mutual Fund Performance," *Journal of Business* 29, pt. 2 (January 1966): 119-38.

_____. "Security Prices, Risk and Maximal Gains from Diversification: Reply," *Journal of Finance* 21 (December 1966): 743-44.

_____. "Comparative Analysis of Mutual Fund versus Common Stock Performance," *Journal of Business* (January 1966).

_____. "A Linear Programming Algorithm for Mutual Fund Portfolio Selection," *Management Science* 13, no. 7 (March 1967): 499-510.

_____. "A Simplified Model for Portfolio Selection," *Management Science* 9 (January 1963): 277-93.

Shelton, John P. "The Value Line Contest: A Test of the Predictability of Stock-Price Changes," *Journal of Business* 11 (July 1967): 251-69.

Simon, Julian J. "Does Good Portfolio Management Exist?" *Management Science* (February 1969).

Smidt, Seymour. "A New Look at the Random Walk Hypothesis," *Journal of Financial and Quantitative Analysis* 3, no. 3 (September 1968): 235-61.

Smith, Keith V. "A Transition Model for Portfolio Revision," *Journal of Finance* 22, no. 4 (September 1967): 425-39.

_____. "Stock Prices and Economic Indexes for Generating Efficient Portfolios," *Journal of Business* (July 1969).

_____. "Needed: A Dynamic Approach to Investment Management," *Financial Analysts Journal* 22, no. 3 (May-June 1967): 115-17.

_____, and Dennis A Tito. "Risk-Return Measures of Ex Post Portfolio Performance," *Journal of Financial and Quantitative Analysis* 4, no. 4 (December 1969): 449-71.

Smith, Randall D. "Short Interest and Stock Market Prices," *Financial Analysts Journal* 24, no. 6 (November-December 1968): 151-54.

Soldofsky, Robert M. "Yield-Risk Performance Measurement," *Financial Analysts Journal* 24, no. 5 (September-October 1968): 130-39.

Treynor, Jack, William W. Priest, Lawrence Fisher, and Catherine A. Higgins. "Using Portfolio Composition to Estimate Risk," *Financial Analysts Journal* 24, no. 5 (September-October 1968): 93-100.

————, and Kay K. Mazuy. "Can Mutual Funds Outguess the Markets.?" *Harvard Business Review* 44, no. 4 (July-August 1966): 131-36.

————, "How to Rate Management of Investment Funds," *Harvard Business Review* 43, no. 1 (January-February 1965): 63-75.

————. "Discussion: The Performance of Mutual Funds in the Period 1945-1964," *Journal of Finance* 23 (May 1968): 418-19.

Van Horne, James C., and George G.C. Parker. "The Random-Walk Theory: An Empirical Test," *Financial Analysts Journal* 23, no. 6 (November-December 1967): 87-92.

Wallich, Henry. "What Does the Random Walk Hypothesis Mean to Security Analysts?" *Financial Analysts Journal* 24, no. 2 (March-April).

Wallingford, Buckner A. "A Survey and Comparison of Portfolio Selection Models," *Journal of Finance and Quantitative Analysis* 2, no. 2 (June 1967): 85-100.

Walter, J.E. "Dividend Policies and Common Stock Prices," *Journal of Finance* (March 1956): 29-41.

————. "Dividend Policy: Its Influence on the Value of the Enterprise," *The Journal of Finance* (May 1963).

Way, Peter F. "Forecasting by Probabilities," *Financial Analysts Journal* 24, no. 2 (March-April 1968): 35.

Welles, Chris. "The Beta Revolution: Learning to Live with Risk," *Institutional Investor* (September 1971): 21 ff.

Wendt, Paul F. "Current Growth Stock Valuation Methods," *Financial Analysts Journal* 21, no. 2 (March-April 1966): 91-103.

West, Richard R. "Mutual Fund Performance and the Theory of Capital Asset Pricing: Some Comments," *Journal of Business* 41 (April 1968): 230-34.

Whiteall, David. "A Simulation Model for Estimating Earnings," *Financial Analysts Journal* 24, no. 6 (November-December 1968): 115-18.

Whitebeck, Volkert S., and Manown Kisor, Jr. "A New Tool in Investment Decision-Making," *Financial Analysts Journal* 19, no. 3 (May-June 1963): 55-62.

Winthrop, John. "Layman's View of Computer Power," *Financial Analysts Journal* 25, no. 5 (September-October: 101-103.

Wippern, Ronald F. "Financial Structure and the Value of the Firm," *Journal of Finance* 21, no. 4 (December 1966): 615-25.

Ying, C.C. "Stock Market Prices and Volume of Sales," *Econometrica* 34 (July 1966): 676-85.

Zakon, Alan J., and James C. Pennypacker. "An Analysis of the

Advance-Decline as a Stock Market Indicator," *Journal of Financial and Quantitative Analysis* 3, no. 3 (September 1968): 299-314.

Zeikel, Arthur. "Coordinating Information," *Financial Analysts Journal* 25, no. 2 (March-April 1969): 119-123.

Newspapers, Business Magazines, and Publications of Other Organizations

Chase, Richard A., Jr. et al. *Computer Applications in Investment Analysis.* Hanover, New Hampshire: Amos Tuck School of Business Administration, Dartmouth College, 1966.

Cootner, Paul. "Technician's Contribution in Selecting Undervalued Stocks." *The Commercial and Financial Chronicle.* September 16, 1965.

Heberton, William B. "Lessons Learned from Random Selection." Drexel Harriman Ripley, March 1969.

"Can an Earnings Decline Indicate Progress?" Drexel Harriman Ripley, July 15, 1968.

"The Magic of the Computer." *Forum for Institutional Investors.* Drexel Harriman Ripley, January 1969.

"Will Size Affect Market Performance?" Drexel Harriman Ripley, July 18, 1968.

Howard, Godfrey G. "The Use of Computers in Investment Analysis." *The Commercial and Financial Chronicle.* December 8, 1966.

Investor Management Sciences, Inc. *Compustat Information Manual* (Denver, Colorado, 1966).

Kahl, Alfred L. "Computers and Investment Management." *Georgia Business* 27, no. 12 (June 1968).

Thomas, Dana L. "Electronic Investing Computers Are Making Decisions." *Barron's.* August 14, 1967.

"Computers and Investors: Electronic Brains are Making Remarkable Advances in Security Analysis." *Barron's.* June 22, 1964.

"Where the Action Is, Computers Have Increased Volatility and Risk in the Stock Market." *Barron's.* August 28, 1967.

Unpublished Materials

Ahlers, David M., and Marc H. Staglitz. "The Effect of Institutional Arrangements for Decision Making on the Selection of Portfolios."

Presentation to the Seminar on the Analysis of Security Prices. University of Chicago, November, 1968.

Benishay, H. "Determinants of Variability in Earnings Price Ratios of Corporate Equity." Unpublished Ph.D dissertation, University of Chicago, 1960.

Baumol, William J. "Problems in the Construction of Stock Valuation Models," Financial Research Center, Princeton University, Date unknown.

Peggy Heim, Burton Malkiel, and Richard E. Quant. "Earnings Retention and Growth of the Firm." Financial Research Center, Princeton University, 1968.

Blume, Marshall. "The Assessment of Portfolio Performance." Unpublished Ph.D Dissertation, University of Chicago, 1968.

Brealy, Richard A. "Some Implications of the Comovement of Company Earnings." *Presentation to the Seminar on the Analysis of Security Prices*. University of Chicago, November, 1968.

Breen, William. "A Note on Portfolio Simulations and the Value of Forward Information," *Presentation to the Seminar on the Analysis of Security Prices* . University of Chicago, November 1968.

Davidson, Sidney. "Earnings per Share: The Investor's Dream and the Analysts' Nightmare," *Presentation to the Seminar on the Analysis of Security Prices*, University of Chicago, November 1968.

Davis, J. V. "The Adjustment of Stock Prices to New Information." Unpublished Ph.D. Dissertation, Cornell University, 1967.

Fisher, Eric. "More about Stability of Measures of Volatility of Individual Stocks," *Presentation to the Seminar on the Analysis of Security Prices*, University of Chicago, November 1968.

Fisher, Lawrence. "Effectiveness of Diversification: Some Further Results." *Presentation to the Seminar on the Analysis of Security Prices*. University of Chicago, November 1968.

Gaumnitz, Jack E. "Investment Diversification under Uncertainty: An Examination of the Number of Securities in a Diversified Portfolio." Unpublished Ph.D Dissertation, Stanford University, 1967.

Gruber, Martin Jay. "Determinants of Common Stock Prices." Unpublished Ph.D. Dissertation, Columbia University, 1966.

Kittner, Robert H. "The Performance of Price-Indifferent Security Selection Criteria," *Presentation to the Seminar on the Analysis of Security Prices*, University of Chicago, November, 1968.

Leland, Hayne Ellis. "Dynamic Portfolio Theory." Unpublished Ph.D. Dissertation, Harvard University, May 1968.

McWilliams, James. "Prices, Earnings and P/E Ratios." *Presentation to the Workshops on the Use of Computers in Financial Analysis*. Park Sheraton Hotel, New York City, December 9, 1965.

Muhlbach, Walter F. *Financial Analysis and the Corporate Annual Report* Washington, D.C.: American University, 1967.

Owen, J. "An Investor in the Stock Market." Unpublished Ph.D. Dissertation, Harvard University, 1966.

Peterson, Donald M. "Stock Market Forecasting—Skill or Chance" (MBA Thesis, Wharton, University of Pennsylvania, 1962).

Pratt, Shannon. "Relationship between Variability of Past Returns and Levels of Future Returns for Common Stocks, 1926-1960." *Presentation at the Management Science Conference*. Atlanta, Georgia, Fall, 1969.

Robichek. Alexander A. "The Impact of Risk on the Value of Securities." *Presentation at the Institute for Quantitative Research in Finance*, San Francisco, California, October 10, 1968.

Synnott, Thomas W. "Time-Series Analysis for Investment Decisions." *Presentation to the Seminar on the Analysis of Security Prices*, University of Chicago, November 1968.

Thornber, Hodson E. "A Workable Procedure of Optimizing the Value for Portfolio." *Presentation to the Seminar on the Analysis of Security Prices*, University of Chicago, November 1968.

Way, Peter F. "Direct Involvement of the Analyst with the Computer, Why and How It Is Done," *Address to the Financial Analysts Federation Convention*, New York City, May 26, 1966.

Zarnowitz, Victor. "Earnings Forecasts and Stock Prices: A Study in Quarterly Time Series," *Presentation to the Seminar on the Analysis of Security Prices*, University of Chicago, May 1968.

Index

Index

About the Author

Donald M. Peterson is a consultant to financial institutions, including Marine Midland Banks, New York, and Computer Directions Advisors, Silver Spring, Maryland, providing research and computer-aided services to his clients. In addition, he is portfolio manager for private accounts and is Chairman of the Dommarel Foundation. He has been a Supervisor Consultant with Lybrand, Ross Bros. & Montgomery and a Senior Project Specialist with RCA, both jobs involving computer-based systems for decision-making. Dr. Peterson received the Bachelor of Mechanical Engineering and Master of Science Degrees from Rensselaer Polytechnic Institute, the MBA in Finance from the Wharton School of Finance and Commerce of the University of Pennsylvania, and the Ph.D. from The American University, Washington, D.C. He is a member of The Institute of Management Sciences and the Computer Applications Committee of the New York Society of Security Analysts, and he is registered as an investment advisor with the Securities and Exchange Commission.